EMOTIONAL
FREEDOM
TECHNIQUES **EFT**
**FOR**
**CHRISTIANS**
**52** TAPPING DEVOTIONS
EFT FOR CHRISTIANS SERIES, BOOK 4

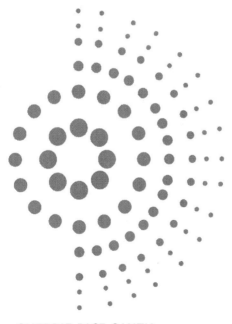

SHERRIE RICE SMITH, R.N. (RETIRED) CERTIFIED EFT PRACTITIONER
WITH CATHY CORBETT REILING & RONDA ROLPH STONE

True Potential
REACH THE WORLD

All scripture verses used in this book, unless otherwise noted, are from the New International Version.

EMOTIONAL FREEDOM TECHNIQUES—EFT FOR CHRISTIANS 52 Tapping Devotions

Cover and Interior Page design by True Potential, Inc.

ISBN: 978-1-943852-70-3 (paperback)
ISBN: 978-1-943852-71-0 (e-book)
Library of Congress Control Number: 2017957610

True Potential
REACH THE WORLD

True Potential, Inc.
PO Box 904, Travelers Rest, SC 29690
www.truepotentialmedia.com

Printed in the United States of America.

# Dedication

As always I dedicate this book first and foremost to my Lord Jesus Christ, my Savior and my Healer Who does marvelous things on my behalf, now and eternally.

To Brad: Thank you for giving me the space, time and resources to write as God asks me to do. God truly gave me a gift when He gave me you!

To Joy: Thank you for helping me edit, correcting with your red teacher's pen, all my spelling, grammar and punctuation!

To the Christian EFT Community: Thank you for your loving support. There are many who send me messages to encourage me to continue this tapping path. I'm grateful for each and every one of you and I pray for you daily, too.

# Please read the following Disclaimer before proceeding further.

The information presented in this book, including, ideas, suggestions, exercises, techniques, and other materials, is educational in nature and is provided only as general information and is not medical or psychological advice. This book is solely intended for the reader's own self-improvement and is not meant to be a substitute for medical or psychological treatment and does not replace the services of licensed health care professionals.

This book contains information regarding an innovative healing method called Emotional Freedom Techniques or EFT, which is considered part of the field of complementary and alternative medicine. EFT seeks to address stressors and imbalances within the person's energy system, as well as the energetic influence of thoughts, beliefs, and emotions on the body. EFT is intended to balance an individual's energy with a gentle tapping procedure. The general premise of EFT is that the flow and balance of the body's electromagnetic and subtler energies are essential for physical, spiritual, and emotional health, and for fostering well-being.

Although EFT appears to have promising emotional, spiritual, and physical health benefits, EFT has yet to be fully researched by the Western academic, medical, and psychological communities. Therefore EFT may be considered experimental. The reader agrees to assume and accept full responsibility for any and all risks associated with reading this book and using EFT. If the reader has any concerns or questions about whether or not to use EFT, the reader should consult with his/her licensed health care professional. If the reader inadvertently experiences any emotional distress or physical discomfort using EFT, the reader is advised to stop and to seek professional care, if appropriate.

Publishing of the information contained in this book is not intended to create a client-practitioner or any other type of professional relationship between the reader and the authors. The authors do not make any guarantee that the reader will receive or experience the same results described in this book. Further, the authors do not make any guarantee, warranty, or prediction regarding the outcome of an individual using EFT as described herein for any particular purpose or issue.

While references and links to other resources are provided in good faith, the accuracy, validity, effectiveness, completeness, or usefulness of any information herein, as with any publication, cannot be guaranteed.

By continuing to read this book the reader agrees to forever, fully release, indemnify, and hold harmless, the authors, and others associated with the publication of this book from any claim or liability and for any damage or injury of whatsoever kind or nature which the reader may incur arising at any time out of or in relation to the reader's use of the information presented in this book. If any court of law rules that any part of the Disclaimer is invalid, the Disclaimer stands as if those parts were struck out.

**BY CONTINUING TO READ THIS BOOK, YOU AGREE TO ALL OF THE ABOVE**

# Contents

# Preface

Suggestions for Devotional Use

The way I suggest you use these devotions is this: Read one of the devotions a week and use it as homework throughout that week. Mull over the Scriptures cited. Cogitate on the thoughts presented. Practice the tapping skills suggested. I would do all these things while tapping!

We, the authors, have tried to give you enough variations in devotional styles to keep you busy for an entire year. Personal stories, private thoughts, physiological lessons and Scriptural instructions are all used. It's quite a mix here!

Finish the book in 52 weeks, and then turn around and do them again because by next year at this time through the Holy Spirit's work in you and the tapping you do, you will most likely be a better version of yourself in Christ than you are today! As with continued Scripture reading, new thoughts and lessons pop up with each subsequent reading of the material.

Many emotionally hurting people cannot *feel*. Their emotions are entirely shut off and shut down because of deep abuse. Remember, as you read these devotions, to concentrate on how you *feel*. This is after all – **Emotional** Freedom Techniques!

Much of the time, the pain you now encounter entered your body and mind through a *feeling*. Feelings are how the body and the mind communicate. It is not unusual to see that when emotional pain isn't dealt with (and in our case tapped on), it can eventually transfer itself to physical pain or a physical problem. The emotional psyche wants attention, and like a toddler, it will get that attention one way or another.

While some of the "action" pieces of the devotions may sound alike, and they are that way purposefully, as my ulterior motive in repeating those thoughts to you is for you to learn to ask specific questions of the Holy Spirit while tapping. He is faithful to answer, but sometimes not knowing what we want to know, what we want to change or how to couch the question creates the block for us.

Perhaps, right here, right now, I will create another more thorough list of questions you can keep as a reference as you pray and tap. Once you learn how to get specific in your tapping, you will find it is more efficient and more effective than you ever imagined EFT to be.

The list literally is endless, but I hope this cataloging of different questions will stimulate you to understand what exactly to ask our Lord while tapping and praying to find your own personal clearing material and avenue.

Because I wanted to keep the devotions relatively short, I couldn't incorporate all the possible questions into each one, covering all the tapping contingencies, so here are more questions for you to muse on.

**Here is the list of possible questions:**

- What adult taught me that belief?
- From whom did I witness a similar attitude?
- What were the circumstances around that event?
- What age was I?
- What was I wearing that day?
- Where was I when that event happened?
- Who else was with me at the time?
- What were they wearing?
- How did their facial expression look?
- What did they say?
- What did I hear? Any words? Any noises?
- What did I say to myself when this happened?
- Was there a smell involved?
- What colors do I remember? Other visuals you recall?
- How do I feel NOW about that incident?
- What do I tell myself today about what happened?
- What meaning does that memory hold today?
- Did I make a vow or a promise to God or someone else?
- What do I want changed in my life? What might that look like to me?
- How will I know when change this happens?

- What stops me from changing/getting what I want/need?
- What do I feel in my body right now? Where is the feeling located?
- What part of life is holding me back?
- What is one of my earliest memories about this?
- When was an earlier time I felt this way?
- What emotional block do I have around this that doesn't allow me to heal?
- Who does this event remind me of?

For you who may have picked up this devotional book as a curiosity, or perhaps for those of you who want a review, the following pages give a quick explanation of what Emotional Freedom Techniques (EFT) or Tapping.

# Tapping Explanation

EFT is a relatively new healing modality happened upon by a Stanford trained engineer named Gary Craig. It is all predicated on God's created physiology and how our body heals.

When we stub our toe or cut our finger, do we run to the doctor or pharmacy to get his/her advice or to purchase half a dozen pills to fix the injury? Instead, we ice our injury after washing out the wound and cover it with a bandage to protect it while God heals it. Most often we never think about the healing process again. It just happens!

While this is an over-simplification of healing, especially when dealing with severe diseases and chronic illnesses, EFT is often the ice or the bandage to our bodies. What most often interferes and causes our diseases and illnesses are our emotions – they impact the healing, and before that the emotions impact whether we come down with the illness at all. This is the basis of the study of epigenetics – our negative emotions turn on certain disease genes whereas research appears to be showing that good emotional health keeps those illness genes turned off, maintaining our health.

God has imparted to us an innate healing ability through His created physiology. We need to learn and use what He has given us!

In other words, if we can get our emotions, stress reactions and our childhood perceptions, which increase our internal stress without us even knowing it, out of the way, our body can sometimes heal itself, no matter what the problem. Now, we Christians know it really is God healing us, but our bodies can do this without our thinking about it.

One example is this: Hormones, such as adrenaline and cortisol, rise when we are stressed. It is a well-known fact that chronic elevations of these hormones, and others, will destroy our organs, creating chronic illnesses. When done efficiently and efficaciously, EFT can help contain and lower these hormone levels allowing another adrenal hormone, DHEA, level to rise. DHEA is the hormone we want roaming our body at high levels, as it rejuvenates and renews our cells, helping with the healing process. Cortisol long-term damages; DHEA long-term heals, as these have an inverse relationship – when one is up, the other is down. We want DHEA up and cortisol down as much as possible for as long as possible in life.

There appear to be many other physiological mechanisms underpinning how EFT works. Some are conjecture, but others can be seen in fMRI studies.

Tapping is a technique whereby we literally tap with our fingertips on some face and upper body acupressure points to drop our stress levels, which include, very importantly, neutralizing the emotions around all our early childhood traumas and abuses.

There are now over 100 studies showing the efficacy of EFT. It tends to work pretty well, once we take the time to learn to do the technique well. EFT has a learning curve.

EFT is also a self-help tool. Once we learn it and once we have neutralized any major traumatic events in our lives (with the help of a certified EFT Practitioner), we can continue to work on older memories that cause underlying subconscious stress or stresses from our daily life in general.

In my original *EFT for Christians* book published in 2015, you will find a 64-page tapping manual that explains in full detail exactly *how* to do this tapping technique. Before you attempt any devotions in this volume and in order for you to benefit from these devotions, I highly suggest you have a complete and thorough understanding of the tapping process..

# More EFT Tools

As you all know, these *EFT for Christians* books aren't written for me, but they are written for you, the reader. Consider purchasing extra copies for your family and friends or perhaps giving a book to your pastor or local healing counselor. Putting a copy in your local church library for circulation gets the EFT word out, too. I've taken to keeping a few copies in the backseat of my car and placing a copy in those neighborhood Free Libraries boxes that seem to be popping up all over the country.

I'm committed to spreading EFT into the entire Christian world, so contact me at EFTforChristians@gmail.com when you become interested in obtaining bulk lot copies of these books. Churches and study groups have requested discounted copies.

This particular book is the result of my listening and replying to questions and suggestions on the EFT for Christians Discussion Group page on Facebook (https://www.facebook.com/groups/352652964926202/). Several of the gals on this board requested Christian EFT Devotions. I had nothing to offer them, so God helped me write a goodly number of them.

Steve Spillman, my book publisher (http://www.truepotentialmedia.com/ ), suggested we go ahead and create a book around these newly written devotions.

So, as we moved ahead with the help of Ronda Rolph Stone and Cathy Corbett Reiling, I pray you find these devotions useful and thought provoking, not only in your own spiritual journey but also in tapping journey.

You have heard me say it repeatedly - try EFT on any negative emotions/sensations or any physical problems that creep up on you. You have little to lose by tapping, except a bit of time, and that is indeed not wasted if you use prayer while you tap. Our prayer time is so precious to both our Lord and us that we should savor every minute of it..

As always, if you have any questions about EFT, and Christian tapping, in particular, you can find me either on Facebook (https://www.facebook.com/groups/352652964926202/) in the EFT for Christians Discussion Group, which you are welcome to join, or email me at EFTforChristians@gmail.com.

For other instructional ideas to assist you to learn how to use Christian EFT effectively, I have created 35 or more EFT for Christians YouTube Videos that you can find here: https://www.youtube.com/channel/UCmxsHG9CFSWot3rDZac2rSw. Please subscribe to this YouTube Channel so that you will be notified when I post new Christian EFT videos!

My EFT for Christians website is found here: http://EFTforChristians.com . There is a "resource" tab on the top menu. You can find my Facebook group on that page, along with a 6-7 page Internet reference link whereby I have collected EFT science related articles for you to read covering all the different areas God has impacted as to how EFT works, many of them research articles.

My prayer for you, and I do pray for you daily, is God grants you the healing you so desire. As He does this, I pray you will be brought into a closer walk with our Savior, Jesus, as He walks us to our eternal heavenly home.

Be blessed in the Risen Christ!
Sherrie Rice Smith
Author of the *EFT for Christians* book series

# 1

# Annoying People

*Be kind and compassionate to one another, forgiving each other, just as in Christ God forgave you.*

Ephesians 4:32

Have you noticed that most people around you love to recount all their life's woes and problems, in detail? You have friends who know you will listen; therefore, you are the one who they call at unpleasant hours and at the most inconvenient times to unload all their day's work and personal issues.

How to handle these situations once plagued me. I hated to say I didn't have time to listen, but I really didn't want to give audience to a long litany of complaints. The tirades wore me out!

God gave me a solution when He gave me tapping! It's a terrific compromise. Most of my friends know I do EFT and some of them have joined me. Even those who don't routinely tap often will play my tapping "game." It's the only way I will listen to their catalog of complaints.

When the phone rings and I hear the words, "It's been an awful day," I reply with this comment, "I will be happy to listen, but we are both going to tap while you talk, ok?" Some readily agree. Others reluctantly do so, and I often slip into the conversation, "You're tapping, right?" to assure myself they are continuing to do so.

There's an amazing physiological mechanism going on during the tapping, even for one who doesn't believe it works or understands how it works. Since tapping quiets the emotions around life's events, just talking and tapping will counteract the negativities your friend *feels* about his/her day. The emotions seem to just melt away. Usually, by the end of the phone call, my friends will say, "Well, I *feel* so much better just talking about this," when I know the talking didn't do the trick, tapping did!

For you, tapping while your friend whines and complains keeps you from empathetically picking up and absorbing all their emotions while they tell you their story. We all need to be Teflon friends, not Velcro friends! Listen, be kind and encouraging, and pray, but don't become so wrapped up in your friends' stories that your own stress level becomes elevated, compromising your own health.

Thought: Have a strategy for the next time frenzied friends phone you! Put a sticky note near your phone that says, "Tap" to remind you to do just that when the negative ranting begins.

Action: Use the above advice! Better yet, teach your friends to use this advice. If your spouse understands why you tap, or he/she uses EFT, when words within household conversations become a bit heated, start tapping! Teach your children to do this too. It is amazing how many arguments my husband and I have adverted by just tapping (right to each other's face) when the words coming out of the other's mouth begins to trigger us. EFT is a mighty pacifying tool!

*Prayer: Lord, way too often I find myself triggered by what others are saying. I know it is my own selfish desires or memories doing much of the triggering, and for that, I ask Your forgiveness right here, right now. Please help me to settle down by tapping, knowing the words others use usually have little or nothing to do with me. Unlock for me those memories bringing them into submission to You. In Jesus' name, Amen.*

Further meditation: Proverbs 29:11, Proverbs 15:1, 1 Timothy 2:8, Ephesians 4:2

*Sherrie Rice Smith*

18

2

# Arise, Shine, for Our Light Has Come

Arise, shine, for your light has come,
and the glory of the LORD RISES UPON YOU.
See, darkness covers the earth
and thick darkness is over the peoples,
but the LORD RISES UPON YOU
and his glory appears over you.
Nations will come to your light,
and kings to the brightness of your dawn.

Isaiah 60:1-3

Our Light is Jesus. Scripture has made that point abundantly clear (John 8:12, John 12:35, Ephesians 5:14).

What does light do for us? It dispels darkness. In our emotional and physical selves, we live in the darkness of distress and sin. We see no light. We have all heard of those who suffer from *feeling* depressed. They speak of overbearing darkness. No hope, no power, no joy, just darkness from which there appears to be no escape.

Verse 2 of this text speaks of the Lord's glory appearing over us. How can both darkness and glory live together? They cannot, as they are opposites. During Jesus' Transfiguration, the apostles fell on their faces because they couldn't stand the brightness of Jesus' glory. Light and glory attract others who feel only darkness.

In the gift of tapping, God the Father dispels our personal darkness. As we confess our sins, He clears our souls. The light of the Holy Spirit is thus freed to shine through us.

19

When God's glory rises over us and appears on us, the Light of Christ, our light, will shine out into the world. Light cannot be hidden.

Let the light of EFT break over you by the grace of our Lord so that God's Holy Light shines brightly showing all who know you the way to salvation through Christ Jesus.

In the same way, let your light shine before others that they may see your good deeds and glorify your Father in heaven (Matthew 5:16).

**Thought:** What dark emotional splotch has God removed for you via His gift of tapping? Often with tapping, we will find little personal habits change or perhaps disappear with continued tapping. When these disappear, God is changing you from the inside out. Praise and thank Him for that healing!

*Prayer: Lord, as we continue our tapping in You keep us focused on the Light of Christ, allowing that Light to penetrate the darkness of our inner emotional pain, clearing it for Your glory and praise. As we thank you for all you have done for us, we ask this in Jesus' holy name. Amen.*

**Further meditation:** Luke 11:34-35, 1 Peter 2:9, Matthew 4:16, John 8:12, 1 John 1:5-9

*Sherrie Rice Smith*

# 3

# Belief

I believe in God the Father Almighty, Maker of heaven and earth.

And in Jesus Christ his only Son our Lord; who was conceived by the Holy Ghost, born of the Virgin Mary, suffered under Pontius Pilate, was crucified, dead, and buried; he descended into hell; the third day he rose again from the dead; he ascended into heaven, and sits on the right hand of God the Father Almighty; from thence he shall come to judge the quick and the dead.

I believe in the Holy Ghost; the holy Christian Church; the communion of saints; the forgiveness of sins; the resurrection of the body; and the life everlasting.

Apostle's Creed

It is understood that the Apostle's Creed was written during Council of Milan in 390 A.D. Different versions have appeared, but this article of faith is one of the central statements of our Christian dogma.

Whether you came to believe these basic tenets early during Sunday school, or later as a baptized adult isn't important. What is important is whether you believe the Creed as written or whether you have any doubts about any part of it.

We all carry around limiting beliefs that were formed during childhood. Most often those beliefs aren't our opinions but viewpoints of someone else – conclusions we heard voiced often enough to think them to be true. What if those sentiments hold no validity even though we believed those presuppositions because they came from an authoritarian figure?

Since God is our Spirit of Truth, allow the Holy Spirit to clarify what He wants you to believe. He is the One Jesus left here on earth to help us through life.

Thoughts/Action: Begin tapping on your favorite tapping spot. Repeat the Apos-

21

tle's Creed several times, out loud, as you pay close attention to what your body is *feeling*. Is there a specific statement where your body *reacts*? Close your eyes, keep tapping, and ask the Holy Spirit what that bodily *reaction* means. What does the *feeling* remind you of?

As with our usual protocol, use the information that God has provided and tap through whatever memories or incidents He gives you to clear up. Remember, your body is a messenger bringing you information about how you *feel* directly from your own subconscious mind. The Holy Spirit facilitates the delivery from our inner mind to our conscious mind. Did the tapping change your thoughts/beliefs?

**Prayer:** *Lord Jesus, I want to believe everything about Who You are and what You have done for us as our Creator, Redeemer, and Guide. Please clarify for me any misunderstanding or unbelief around any core tenet of Christianity. I crave peace and assurance that only You can give me here on earth. Help me stand solidly on the Rock of my salvation which is You. I ask this in Your name. Amen.*

**Further meditation:** Romans 10:9, Genesis 1, John 16:13, John 14:26

*Sherrie Rice Smith*

# 4

# Breathing

In His hand is the life of every creature and the breath of all mankind.

Job 12:10

Breathing is essential to life. We breathe, or we die. There is no in between here.

Rarely do I pay any attention to my breathing. Do you? It is a natural process God instilled in us at birth. It takes no effort, but breathe we must if we are to continue our existence here on earth.

Often the Holy Spirit is equated to wind or air, like breathing. He is essential to our spiritual life. It is He Who is in control of our emotional life. He understands what lies in our heart, be that something good or something hateful.

I often teach, and I specifically do this when tapping with clients, to breathe deeply. It engages the parasympathetic nervous system helping to relax us. Deep breaths calm us. It clears our mind by allowing blood to return to our pre-frontal cortex where decisions are made.

The Holy Spirit functions the same way in our spiritual life. He takes over if we allow Him to do so, assisting us with important life decisions, relaxing us to know we are held in the almighty hands of the Father. Our life is literally entwined in God.

When emotional pain encompasses us, it interferes in this relationship with our Lord. Literally, we breathe shallowly, like we are awaiting the next wave of distress. Fear holds us back from taking a deep breath in the Lord Jesus, allowing Him to carry our pain.

Action: Try it now. Breathe deeply into your belly, slowly for 7 seconds. Hold your breath now for 2 seconds, and then slowly blow out that air for another 7 seconds. Repeat this exercise 5 times. Can you *feel* your body relaxing? Do you *feel* your mind clearing? Try doing this exercise before you begin tapping. That is how it *feels* to allow the Father to carry your burdens. He has your life in His hands, gently holding you. Breathe, relax, He has this all planned out for your good.

There is also another technique called "Touch and Breathe" whereby you lightly touch and hold, not tap, the acupuncture points and take a deep breath like described above. This is a quieter process. Often this is useful for older people who dislike or cannot stand the actual tapping, or for those who have some kind of tactile issue. It can also be helpful to use before sleeping, as it is less stimulating.

***Prayer:*** *Lord God, You hold my life in Your hands. You know everything about me. I breathe because You have given me the capacity to do so. My dependence is on You alone. Help me to feel You carrying my burdens. Send Your Holy Spirit into my being, teaching me how to let life go, allowing You to run it to my betterment. I ask this in Jesus' name. Amen.*

**Further Meditation:** Psalm 33:6, Isaiah 42:5, Isaiah 2:22, Job 32:8

*Sherrie Rice Smith*

# 5

# Calamity

**I call on the LORD IN MY DISTRESS, and he answers me.**

**Psalm 120:1**

In today's world, bad news abounds everywhere. It never seems to end. We *feel* assaulted from every angle in life, a constant barrage of woe and hardship, but God clearly tells us in Scripture that He has our back.

In all that terror and fright, He stands with us, and He knows our plight. He is never far away. Call upon the Lord, and He will comfort you in any peril.

Anxiety and fear are as catching as a cold or flu sweeping through an office in a flash, leaving the place looking like a hospital ward. We literally feed off other people's emotions. We can *feel* what they *feel*, often over long distances. It's our empathetic mirror neurons kicking in, doing their job for us.

What happens when that connection is all negative? Often we get swept up in the wave of the moment, so overwhelmed we forget God is still in control.

This is a perfect time to tap, allowing God to settle down your sympathetic nervous system. When others *feel* you quiet down, their mirror neurons kick in, and they calm down. It is an excellent witness of the Lord's peace that you can offer those around you. *Feel* God holding you in the palm of His hand during these times of calamity and distress. He has it all under control!

**Thoughts:** Where were you during 911, John and Robert Kennedy's and Martin Luther King's assassinations, Columbine or the Challenger explosion? Looking back on those experiences what do you *feel* right now? If you *feel* any residual distress around those events or around any other catastrophe in your life, such as death, accident, natural disaster or a medical problem, consider tapping on those, too. We learn our neural patterns in layers, often setting us up for a deeper usually negative emotional experience with each subsequent event. It may be time to pull out any residual negative memories you have concerning disastrous events in your life, freeing you to move forward in the name of Jesus.

**Prayer:** *Lord, show me all the times in my life where I was deeply moved by events around me. Give me a thorough understanding of what parts of those times I must turn over to you. Let me allow You to calm my heart and soul to feel You holding me close to Your heart. Give me constant reassurance that You are with me wherever I go. In Jesus' name, I pray. Amen.*

**Further Meditation:** Romans 5:3, 2 Samuel 22:7, Psalm 40:12, Nahum 1:7

*Sherrie Rice Smith*

# 6

# Capturing Thoughts

The weapons we fight with are not the weapons of the world. On the contrary, they have divine power to demolish strongholds. We demolish arguments and every pretension that sets itself up against the knowledge of God, and we take captive every thought to make it obedient to Christ.

2 Corinthians 10: 4-5

Oh, what wild excursions our thoughts and beliefs can lead us on! They almost look to be scary theme park rides! Some of our subconscious ride themes could be named like these: "The Guilt of No Return," "Mr. I'm Not Good Enough's Adventures" or "Pirates in I'm Not Likeable Land," and, of course, "They're Better than Me Fun House." These mental rides happen before we even enter the theme park. Something triggers us, and off we go, screaming and carrying on as if these amusement park rides are our real life.

God gave us a subconscious mind to protect us. Sometimes it gets overly protective. It memorizes situations that terrified us as a child. Now, as an adult, when we encounter a similar theme, our subconscious mind triggers in us the exact same reaction as it did when we were younger. As adults, we can now protect ourselves. We don't need the constant warnings anymore, but our mind doesn't know this.

Our brain is responding innately to a stimulus on a physiological level when we get emotionally triggered or feel threatened. The unobserved thought (which begins the process) is pondered in the mind, and it will produce chemicals, either positive or negative, based on previous experience, usually in childhood. The body physiologically reacts to the chemical stimulus in a way it interprets as appropriate by producing emotions and feelings.

Apostle Paul knew well about these thoughts and beliefs. He called them " "strongholds," which by definition means "fortified place." He was aware that they needed to be demolished and torn down. Taking thoughts captive to make them obedient to Christ is our spiritual warfare. This allows God to then move in our life. If we have the strongholds (beliefs) and disobedient thoughts running our lives, the wild and crazy emotional theme park is the result.

Do not conform to the pattern of this world, but be transformed by the renewing of your mind. You will be able to test and approve what God's will is-His good, pleasing and perfect will (Romans 12:2). The mind renewal process is an act of our free will.

**Thought:** So how can we halt this insanity and get off these rides and leave the park? God gave us EFT to help us demolish false belief strongholds in our mind.

**Action:** What stray thoughts would you like God to change? What negative thoughts do you think about multiple times a day? Consider applying tapping, a user-friendly fingertip technique, to help you take those thoughts captive. Beliefs absorbed from childhood events are many times running our belief show, dictating what behavior we will exhibit next. The enemy uses these beliefs/strongholds against us. They are actually lies that rise up against the knowledge of God. Taking authority over these lies is the spiritual warfare to which we are called.

So, when you *feel* yourself getting on an unwanted emotional amusement ride, start tapping immediately to calm the body. The more you practice this, the shorter the future rides will be. Often, with continued tapping repetition, you will just choose to skip going at all to the amusement park! God will have transformed your mind and calmed your spirit enough that you now *feel* safe in His arms, emotionally quiet.

***Prayer:*** *Thank you, God, You have given us instructions on how to get off of these emotional roller coasters. Thank You that You created us so that our minds can be renewed and our brains rewired to better live the life that You have prepared for us. Amen.*

**Further Meditation:** Philippians 4:8, Ephesians 4:22-32, Colossians 3:2-4

*Cathy Corbett Reiling*

# 7

# Count it All Joy

**Consider it pure joy, my brothers and sisters, whenever you face trials of many kinds, because you know that the testing of your faith produces perseverance. Let perseverance finish its work so that you may be mature and complete, not lacking anything.**

**James 1:2-4**

No one likes facing trials in life. When we are being tempted to sin or facing mental or physical adversity, it isn't easy, and it takes perseverance to make it through the ordeal. That brand of determination doesn't come from our own efforts. It takes God working in us to persevere in the testing. The Amplified Bible puts it this way: "But let endurance and steadfastness and patience have full play so that you may be people perfectly and fully developed with no defects, lacking in nothing."

How great would that be to *feel* as if nothing is lacking in us? Unfortunately, we don't get there without the heartbreak or temptations. I believe it is a lifelong journey and I'm glad I don't have to have it all together on my own. It is good when the end of a trial comes, and I know the Lord helped me overcome it and brought me to a place where I *feel* I have made it to the other side of the hardship.

But wait, there's more. It seems when one trial ends, another begins, and so goes life. Remember, God is always with us, always ready to equip us for our journey. Keep our eyes on the Prize, which is life in Christ Jesus because it is what we keep our focus on that determines the direction of our trip.

**Thought:** God understands our anguish, distresses, irritations and sorrows. He didn't cause them, but He wants to walk through them with us. Not only is He present with us, but He has also given us another tool called EFT to help us deal with the emotional fall-out that comes along with all of life's problems.

**Action:** We should train ourselves in the moment of emotional upheaval, be it a small molehill or a Mount St. Helens, to tap as soon as we can. Learn to tap on alternate acupuncture points, ones that are clandestine, places such as the back of your hand or fingertips, where no one knows we are tapping. The sooner we tap, the less the chance for the emotions to continue to rise, derailing our entire day. Tap often. Sometimes it only takes a minute or less to defuse an escalating *feeling*. By doing this, you are taking captive every thought that Apostle Paul discusses in 2 Corinthians 10:5, "we take captive every thought to make it obedient to Christ." Don't give satan a foothold in your thoughts or emotions! And watch the joy build in yourself!

*Prayer: Father, forgive me when I feel it is all up to me to get through a trial. Forgive me when I forget You are there all the time. Even though I feel I have failed the test, I know Jesus is my advocate, and because of Him I am found "not guilty."*

**Further Meditation:** Philippians 3:14, Isaiah 12:3-5, Romans 14:7, Romans 15:13

*Ronda Rolph Stone*

# 8

# Despair

No temptation has overtaken you except what is common to mankind. And God is faithful; he will not let you be tempted beyond what you can bear. But when you are tempted, he will also provide a way out so that you can endure it.

1 Corinthians 10:13

There is comfort in this verse! God has everything under control. His omniscience gives us an umbrella under which we can hover, knowing nothing can assail us without God's knowledge and permission. As with Job, God uses adversity to mold and shape us. He has a roadmap for our life with a specific goal at the end of the trials.

I'm going to take a bit of liberty with this verse. I know the word "temptation" is used here, but I believe during the EFT process God never forces healing upon us. We must agree with Him that we want our healing. Some of us fight Him, resist Him, all the while complaining and arguing against emotional change. He is patient. He waits until our tantrum is finished.

The beauty I see in this verse is that God protects us during our healing. He only reveals our memories to us **AS** we can handle them. God never just dumps the entire basket of emotionally rotten apples over our head, telling us to now deal with the mess. He is always gracious and merciful, ever the Father.

Often in tapping, we talk about peeling the onion. This truly is what our Lord does. When we finally agree with Him to begin our tapping journey, He slowly shows us what we must tap on. I know the Holy Spirit prioritizes our tapping; He makes it efficient when we ask Him.

Later in the healing process, when we have allowed Him to heal us of the smaller peripheral things in our life, He will often show us the ugly core – the deep, dark stuff that has been hidden for years by our subconscious mind. God hides it all to protect us.

Keep tapping! Do not despair or be dismayed when these core events reveal themselves. God has it under control. He knows we can now handle the nastier memories and He wishes to provide us with a deeper healing because He has given us tapping to help and to keep us emotionally safe.

**Action:** 99.9% of all events, memories, thoughts, and diseases are tapped the same way! There is no specific way to tap for arthritis or fibromyalgia or sexual abuse (here we just take our time and proceed slower through this quagmire) or anxiousness or any other idea worth tapping. We tap on how we *feel* NOW about whatever it was then allowing the Holy Spirit to reveal memories or events from the past as related to these present emotions.

***Prayer:*** *Lord, I despair of this tapping process. I have felt so awful for so long. I often wonder what lies below the surface. What if I find something devastating to me? All that said, Lord, I want healing now and forever. Help me trust You with me and my emotions. Please get me through this. In Jesus' name. Amen.*

**Further Meditation:** Psalm 91:1-16, 2 Corinthians 12:9, 2 Corinthians 4:8, Psalm 147:3

*Sherrie Rice Smith*

# 9

# Disappointment in Unanswered Prayer

**Let not your heart be troubled, you believe in God, believe also in Me.**

**John 13:27**

In John 13:27 we are plainly told to not be troubled. As humans it is easy to *feel* troubled, but God is serious about the fact that we have Him, so we should leave trouble alone.

Troubled means agitated, disturbed, distressed. I believe God's Word to be true so I believe God means it when He says, "Let not your heart be troubled." So maybe the key here is how to *let God* take our troubles.

Troubles come to us all, but we don't have to allow them to reign over us. God stands in the trouble with us, and He is bigger than any circumstances. We can't prevent troubling things from happening, but with God they can be prevented from agitating and controlling us, as we lean on God, drawing near to Him, asking for His strength and instructions, and then actually doing what He bids.

The event in itself is not the problem – it is our perception and what we think about the event that causes our heart to be troubled. For example – our indoor cat, Oliver, escaped and got outside without our knowing it. Well, it is my husband's cat, and the cat allows me to live here! Anyway, when I realized Oliver was among the missing, my mind began to race, thinking of all the negative things that could happen to him. Oliver the Cat came home safely from his exploits, but in the meantime all the negativity that came to my mind was the greater problem. My mind seemed to exaggerate a million different thoughts about all the trouble Oliver could have encountered while he explored the big wide world to which he was quite unaccustomed. It did provide me with tapping/prayer material!

33

When I pray/tap, I'm not trying to fix myself. I'm talking to God and giving Him my burdens and troubling situations, knowing He is on my side and can bring me through to the other end of the tunnel.

**Thought:** What is troubling you? What are you doing to overcome the thoughts rather than them overcoming you? We shouldn't just make positive confessions pretending that everything is okay when everything around us screams danger. We give our disappointments and anxiousness to God because He can handle it better than we can and is willing to carry it. In that process we permit Him to change our perception of the problem and how we *feel* about it.

**Action:** Always, while praying, tap as you cry out to the Lord God. Allow Him to relieve your emotional state around whatever is bothering you. The tapping often releases us from being overly invested in the outcome. The outcome of every situation is for God to decide, not us. He is in control. Once we disconnect from being too vested in what the future may hold is when the Peace of Christ enters our spirit, and true rest comes.

***Prayer:*** *When bad things happen, or I have an unanswered prayer, and my mind so easily travels to the negative side of things, I deeply trust and love you, Lord. I completely trust and expect You to be with me no matter what happens. When my prayers are not answered in my timing, I deeply trust and love You, Lord, and know that You love me unconditionally.*

**Further Meditation:** Romans 5:3-5, Psalm 12:7, Psalm 13, Nahum 1:7

*Ronda Rolph Stone*

# 10

# Do Not Let the Sun Go Down on Your Anger

**In your anger do not sin. Do not let the sun go down while you are still angry.**

**Ephesians 4:26**

Sherrie Rice Smith recently quoted research showing we have 10 minutes to a 5 hour (some say 10 hour) window to change a memory either positively or negatively. Obviously a negative memory is what makes it emotionally damaging. I wonder if that is why God in His wisdom said to not let the sun go down on our anger.

When we go to bed angry, we are giving the enemy a foothold and allowing our negative emotion to dig a deeper rut, making it harder for us to climb out of the emotional hole. The longer we stay angry, the harder it is on our body. Dr. Chris Aiken, an instructor in clinical psychiatry at the Wake Forest University School of Medicine, says an angry outburst doubles our chances of having a heart attack, triples our chances of having a stroke and weakens our immune system. All of these are good reasons to not go to bed angry. Of course that is so much easier said than done, as we *feel* so justified at times; however, it is a very unhealthy habit that causes havoc in our spirit and body.

Learning to give God our disappointments, fear, anger and other negative emotional responses to what is happening in our life is much healthier and leads to longer, more meaningful life. It isn't easy; it takes a humble heart and mind to not justify our anger. We need to be willing to give God permission to make us willing (and we can actually tap about that willingness, too). We do our part, and God will do the rest. He won't remove from us anything we aren't willing to give Him.

**Thought/Action:** Even if we can't work it out with the person we are having a problem with, we can work it out in our heart with the Lord. We are instructed to be at peace, if possible, with others so far as it depends on us. If not, go for peace in our own heart with our Lord. Tap out the anger with the Lord even if we can't talk it out with the other party.

If you can speak with the other person, try tapping first, giving the anger to God. By tapping we allow the Holy Spirit to minister the peace of God in us by us just taking time to breathe for a few minutes in quietness. Let God release the anger.. We can then speak respectfully to the other person and say what we need to say in love.

**Prayer:** *Father, forgive me for being angry and for taking it to bed with me. That is not how I want to live my life. Forgive me allowing anger to get a foothold. I choose life. Even though I feel angry and it is hard to stop feeling that way, it is not the life I desire. I choose You.*

*Ronda Rolph Stone*

# 11

# Doing

I call with all my heart; answer me, Lord,
and I will obey your decrees.
I call out to you; save me
and I will keep your statutes.
I rise before dawn and cry for help;
I have put my hope in your word.
My eyes stay open through the watches of the night,
hat I may meditate on your promises.

Psalm 119:145-148

As Christians, we often *feel* that "doing" for God equates to "knowing" our God. We still suffer from that pre-saved mentality that we must work to accomplish anything in our life, but our God doesn't require us to work for our salvation or for a relationship with Him. He wants us to *feel* Him and to know Him on a deeply personal level.

We aren't God's slaves; we are His children. He wants the best for us. He wants to love and cherish us, and He wants the same from us toward Himself. You are chosen by the God of the Universe as His very own child.

When you pray, calling on the Lord, do you *feel* His presence? Is He right there beside you? This is the exact thing He desires. He wants you to taste His sweetness.

As you pray and tap, ask God to show you what it means to dwell in His presence quietly, not rushing to do anything for Him.

Tap and *feel* into how God's presence inside you would change your bodily emotions. Let God show you *how* it *feels* to be loved by Him when you hope in Him. Ask Him to wash over you with His love. Allow that love to permeate every cell of your body.

Now, pull in that *feeling* any time you start to overdo life. Settle back and rest in His *feeling* of love for you.

**Action:** What habit or thought interferes with your prayer time? Specifically, tap and ask the Holy Spirit for a direct answer to that question and the answer will come into your mind as a thought. Take some time to tap out any negative thoughts or feelings that keep you from spending quality time with your Lord. Teach yourself to tap while you pray.

***Prayer:*** *Father, you care so deeply for us in every way. We desire to be more like Jesus in our thoughts and actions. Please direct our tapping to clean out our hearts and habits to more resemble Jesus in our lives and to witness to those around us of your glory, mercy and care for us. We ask this in Jesus' name. Amen.*

**Further Meditation:** Micah 6:6-8, Hosea 6:6, Psalm 46:10, Galatians 4:8-9

*Sherrie Rice Smith*

# 12

# Encourage Yourself in the Lord

David was greatly distressed because the men were talking of stoning him; each one was bitter in spirit because of his sons and daughters. But David found strength in the LORD his God.

1 Samuel 30:6

David was in a big mess, and people were angry enough to stone him, and I'm sure he was fearful, yet he found strength in the Lord. In Scriptures about David, I notice that he didn't hold back on crying out to God about what was happening in his life, even though some of what was happening was due to his own poor decisions. Yet David knew that God was the answer to his problems and God would give him the strength he needed. He did not hide from God, he ran to Him when he was in distress.

Psalm 18:6 reads, "In my distress I called to the LORD; I cried to my God for help. From his temple He heard my voice; my cry came before Him, into His ears." David cried out every distressing negative circumstance to God and ended with a "But God" and proceeded to encourage himself that God was his strength and He knew God heard him. In Christian EFT we do this as well with our Setup statement. As a Christian doing EFT, I am not doing EFT to fix myself. I have come to see EFT as a way I talk to God. I see it as a way of giving myself and my problems to God for Him to fix. Like David, I know where my help comes.

Even though David had many flaws and failures in his life, he was still known as a man after God's own heart. He pursued God through an intimate relationship admitting his flaws (confessing his sin), knowing his actions contradicted his desire. Do you run from God when you have sinned or do you run to Him because you have sinned? That is what I want to do, pursue God in spite of my failures. That is when I need God the most.

God desires the same intimate relationship with us as David had. We all fall and make mistakes and sometimes big ones that alter the course of our lives, but God does not turn His back on us. He is waiting for us to come to Him. I want to be a woman after God's own heart.

**Thought:** Tapping helps me accomplish this exact idea. I get all worked up about my mistakes in life, so I use tapping to settle down my emotions, guilt, fear, remorse and then while doing this I tell God how sorry I am, asking His forgiveness. It brings me closer to God.

**Prayer:** *Father, even though I know I fail and fall short, I love You and I desire a deeper relationship with You. Even though I am afraid I have disappointed You, I know You forgive me and want me to come to You. Even though I make mistakes, I choose to encourage myself by running to You.*

**Further Meditation:** Psalm 51, Romans 3:22-25, Proverbs 28:13, Philippians 3:13

*Ronda Rolph Stone*

# 13

# Faith - What an Adventure

**Now faith is confidence in what we hope for and assurance about what we do not see.**

**Hebrews 11:1**

"Faith is the assurance that God is perfecting His design for me when my life's course, once a swift-flowing current seems a stagnant pool. Faith is confidence in God's faithfulness to me in an uncertain world, on an uncharted course, and through an unknown future," penned Dr. Pamela Reeve, professor at Multnomah Bible College and Seminary in Portland, Oregon.

We are told to believe God will provide when we pray because God has it all under control. When we choose steadfast faith, we have all of heaven on our side. Even when we don't get what we request, the Lord gives us something even better because He wants us to grow and He knows what we need to do just that. With steadfast faith, comes steadfast patience, and when we have patience, we have peace and love. Faith works by producing peace and love.

Sometimes faith requires that we shift our position just a bit. While standing by my medicine cabinet the other day looking for something that I couldn't find, I remember a lesson the Lord showed me in that moment. I shifted my position slightly to the left, just a bit, and there was the object I was looking for, plainly in sight. Faith in God, not faith in what we are praying for, will cause us to shift our position so that we can see God. Keeping our eyes fixed on Jesus gets us to our goal. We won't get lost on our way.

Faith is not what I do to get God to respond to me — it is my responding to God in trust, starting with the knowledge that He loves me and I have everything I need in Christ. We make the decision, God won't do that for us, but He will show us our need for Him.

The God kind of faith will prevent doubt from creeping in because doubt closes us off from experiencing God's love and closeness. We should pray for that kind of faith where He is the Author and Finisher of that faith. I used to think my faith was measured by whatever big thing I believed of God in the moment. Instead, God wants us to have His kind of faith which understands how big God is and how big His love is for us. Faith knows "all things" are possible with God, even in such an uncharted, unknown future.

**Thought:** As I use tapping with my prayers, I find my faith growing. God divests me of my need for a particular outcome to the requests I have asked Him. The more of me I let go via EFT, the deeper my relationship to God becomes because I trust Him to do the best for me in my life.

Do you believe God for just a limited number of things or do you believe God for everything? Let Him shift your position to allow you to see Him as everything you need. He can work miracles around all the details in our lives.

**Action:** When we feel disappointed with God, it is often our disappointment with other people who have let us down. Who has disappointed you in life? Find those memories and tap out the negative pieces of them. Let God grant you His peace, growing your faith in His goodness, as you move through life..

***Prayer:*** *Father, even though I forget at times that You don't need me to tell You how to do something, I know You love me and offer me extravagant love which transcends all my needs. You are my Great Adventure, and I choose to live in anticipation of Your Love and Faithfulness.*

**Further Meditation:** Hebrews 11:6-7, Romans 15:13, Galatians 5:6, 1 Corinthians 13:13

*Ronda Rolph Stone*

# 14

# Fake It Until You Make It

Therefore encourage one another and build each other up, just as in fact you are doing.

1 Thessalonians 5:11

The old adage written as this devotion's title actually has a bit of truth to it. There is some physiological underpinning to this idea.

As Christians we *feel* we should always be upbeat, walking around with our church look pasted on our face, like we haven't a care in the world when underneath we are emotionally beat-up and hurting badly.

In reality, our "church face" might actually be helpful. When we smile at another human, we trigger in them as well as in ourselves a hormone called Oxytocin (OT). OT is the active ingredient in Pitocin, the drug pregnant women get to induce labor. OT has other surprising uses – it stimulates a bonding mechanism in us. With each touch, smile, compliment or pat on the back we give another, we release in them a dollop of OT which makes them *feel* better. But even more surprising, that same action releases for us our own dose of OT. We spread good cheer in everyone.

The physiology goes one step further here: Not only do you and your smile recipient receive a dose of OT, but often our mirror neurons kick in here, too, whereby a smile, a kind word or a touch becomes contagious to others around us. Mirror neurons are copycat neurons. We mimic the behaviors of other people. What a wonderful gift to pass around a community – one that releases a bit of OT that brings people closer together!

Encouragement is one of the gifts of the Holy Spirit. In this dark, desperate world filled with pain coming from many directions, what can you do to encourage those around you?

**Thought/Action:** Do you have kind words that help, or are you a nagger who belittles others and tears them down? Can you smile and be cheerful through your own pain, or do you prefer to complain hoping someone will listen to you? Can you non-judgmentally listen to another person while keeping your mouth shut, or must you insert your opinion into the conversation whether you were asked to do so or not? What other habits do you have that detract from those around you from *feeling* loved and important?

Have you considered tapping on those undesirable traits? Pray, and ask the Holy Spirit which of your memories need to be changed to eliminate the negative behavior.

Furthermore, ask Him to help you learn to smile and encourage others even though you may not *feel* like doing so because of the personal pain you carry inside yourself. What events in your life could you tap about to continue to allow God to carry your emotional pain so that your encouraging word and smile to others can become genuine to everyone?

**Prayer:** *Lord, help me to become the Christian you want me to be. Open my heart to others by giving me Your eyes to see them. Let me be an encourager to those around me, building them up in heart and spirit so they can see Your love for them and share that same love with others. In Jesus' name. Amen.*

**Further Meditation:** Proverbs 15:30, Matthew 11:28, Proverbs 14:23, Romans 12:12

*Sherrie Rice Smith*

# 15

# Fear

We wait in hope for the LORD;
he is our help and our shield.
In him our hearts rejoice,
for we trust in his holy name.
May your unfailing love be with us, LORD,
even as we put our hope in You.

Psalm 33:20-22

Fear often reigns fiercely in our darkest moment. Our gut clenches, nausea rises and our throat tightens as we look upon the problem before us. Is God in this moment with us?

We Christians know this is where the rubber meets the road in our belief system. Do we *feel* God with us right now?

Personally, I pray that in that second of danger or worry I will immediately turn to the Lord for comfort and hope. I want my thoughts on Jesus. I need to *feel* the care of the Lord in my deepest fear. We know we serve a great God. He is powerful and mighty. Faith is the key here, but how do we grow our faith to counter our fear and concern?

Fear can be anything – financial, health, family, work, friends or environmental. When something *feels* out of control, and there is nothing we do can fix the problem, fear shows up.

**Thought:** Have you discussed your fears with your Lord while you tap? How does your body *feel* when your fear rises?

**Action:** Take a moment right now, as you pray, to *feel* into your body where fear resides. Tap a few rounds, concentrating on that fear *feeling*. Does a particular

45

memory from the past appear in that feeling? If so, tap out the specifics in that memory, giving all the emotion contained in it back to the Lord. When you are finished tapping, offer your Lord praise and thanksgiving for His hope and salvation.

**Prayer:** *Father God, just as Abram hoped in you, as his fear must have risen when you instructed him to pack up his household and move to an undisclosed location, we ask that You grow our hope and confidence in You as You did in him. Remind us always of Your presence in all areas of our life. Allow us to feel You. In Jesus name. Amen.*

**Further Meditation:** Psalm 33, Genesis 12:1-9, Isaiah 41:10, Psalm 27:1

*Sherrie Rice Smith*

# 16

# Forgiveness

In prayer there is a connection between what God does and what you do. You can't get forgiveness from God without also forgiving others. If you refuse to do your part, you cut yourself off from God's part.

Matthew 6:14-15 (The Message)

God is pretty clear in Scripture. We forgive others, or He won't forgive us. To me, that almost *feels* harsh and heartless.

I used to wonder if God didn't understand! Doesn't He know how badly other people have hurt me? How could He possibly ask me to forgive them? I don't want them to get away with their actions. In hating them, I can continue to punish them, can't I? God had to be crazy. There was no way I could accomplish that leniency towards others.

Yet God takes this all one step further. Not only does He forgive us when we forgive others, but He also forgets our sin!

As He often does, our Lord has once again stepped in to assist us. In our tapping work, we find when we do our work completely, God leads us to forgiveness. He changes our perspective around the person who hurt us. We see the offender in an entirely different light, through eyes of compassion and empathy, probably much like God sees us. It has happened in my life, so I know that EFT does this. Once we have forgiven, the memory's hold on us fades, too. We forgive and to a certain extent, we forget the incident, as we no longer continuously replay it in our mind.

Often it is in that forgiveness that we release anger, resentment, guilt, hatred and rage that is lodged in our body, allowing our body to finally heal. God is so good to us, isn't He?

Thought: Who have you yet to forgive? When you think about this person how

47

does your body *feel?* Write down the description of the *feeling(s).* Be specific, add a few adjectives to each *feeling.* After tapping on these *feelings,* go back and reread your description. How has it changed? Continue tapping until you no longer *feel* any emotional charge about this person. God doesn't require we love our perpetrator; we must not hate them!

**Prayer:** *Heavenly Father, remove from me all the unforgiveness I carry against those who hurt me. You require me to forgive, or you can't forgive me. Show me specifically, Holy Spirit, how to do this. Show me the memories I need to tap to remove my negative emotions, allowing me once and for all to forgive everyone. I ask this in Jesus' name, Amen.*

**Further Meditation:** Matthew 6:9-13, Isaiah 43:25, Hebrews 10:17, Micah 17:18-19

*Sherrie Rice Smith*

# 17

# Free Will

This day I call the heavens and the earth as witnesses against you that I have set before you life and death, blessings and curses. Now choose life, so that you and your children may live and that you may love the Lord your God, listen to his voice, and hold fast to him. For the Lord is your life.

**Deuteronomy 30: 19-20**

God does not force us to make decisions. He did not give birth to robots but children, created in His image. With this gift of free will, we can choose to turn against the very One that gave us this freedom. We are free to choose life, abundance and wholeness or sin and death. He purchased and desires for us to live a blessed life. He does not force us to accept His love.

If we desire to walk in His blessings and live in His abundance, why do we do the opposite? We hear people say they are doing the best that they can. But are they? Another may conclude, "Well that was his/her choice." But, was it truly their choice? Let's consider a few facts before deciding if any of us are doing the best we can or whether choices are truly freely made.

While in a triggered state, the sympathetic nervous system takes command automatically. We have no control over this. Our "fight or flight" kicks in reflexively based on previously learned behavior. The brain reacts to a threat by automatically revving up the sympathetic activity for survival. Up to 70% or more of the blood moves out of the logical forebrain and into the limbs preparing the body to fight or flee. The decision we make when in a calm state is not the same decision we could make when in a stressed mental situation. Safety trumps all other concerns; logical choice goes out the window. We are at the mercy of our earlier, usually childhood, programmed beliefs and conclusions.

While in a stressed state we are not "doing the best that we can" nor can we truly choose. We may be doing the best that we can from that reactionary chemically-driven state, but we aren't doing our best from a place of true God-ordained choice.

We are instructed to "let the peace of Christ rule in our hearts" (Colossians 3:15). In other words, "Let the peace of God be the umpire in your life and actions" or "Let the peace of God act as referee in your emotions and your decisions."

Through prayer and tapping we can once again claim the peace of God and get the clarity needed to make decisions from a place of true choice, so we really can do our best for our Lord.

**Thought/Action:** Through prayer and tapping on the meridian tapping points our body calms down by releasing the parasympathetic quieting chemicals needed to restore the "rest and digest" hormones. We can once again hear what God is saying and decide our course of action peacefully from a place of true free will where we hear God's voice and willingly obey Him.

***Prayer:*** *Thank you, God, for Your peace that passes all understanding. Thank You that You not only give me free will to choose life, but through Your peace I can see which choice to make for my highest purpose. Amen.*

**Further Meditation:** Psalm 25:2, Psalm 64:4, Proverbs 8:10

*Cathy Corbett Reiling*

# 18

# Fruit

**But the fruit of the Spirit is love, joy, peace, forbearance, kindness, goodness, faithfulness, gentleness and self-control.**

**Galatians 5:22-23**

Fruit is a product of something and, in this case, it is a gift of the Holy Spirit. These attributes are not something man made or anything that can be conjured up by will power; they are produced from a relationship with the Holy Spirit.

If you want more love and joy in your life, they are the Fruit of the Holy Spirit of God. If you want more gentleness and self-control in your life, they are the result of walking in the Spirit. The world does not offer these states, it is not from the world that these Fruits exist; they are from the Holy Spirit. The best the world can offer is happiness, which is contingent upon something happening in your life. The Fruit and its attributes are eternal. For example, Nehemiah tells us the Joy of the Lord is our strength. These Fruits produce from the inside out. They are not dependent on the outside circumstances. How can we experience more Fruit from the Spirit of God and less of the world's counterfeit versions?

We deal with so many emotions that take us for uncontrollably wild rides. When our joy is stolen, or we give it up, our strength depletes, and the Fruit is out of reach. With tapping, we take authority over our emotional state that blocks the Fruit from expressing itself. This gets our emotions back in check so we can allow the Spirit's Fruit to reveal itself in and through us. These Fruits are our blessings. They flow from our relationship with God and, like Him, are always available. Tapping is a gardening tool to help the Fruits grow.

It is never too late to decide to take authority over our emotional state. By tapping, we immediately send signals to the brain to calm down. The brain informs the body that the threat is gone. This allows the adrenal glands to release healing hormones to rebuild our immune system. Once calm, we can hear God and operate in His Fruits of the Spirit.

**Thought:** Lying emotions prevent God's Fruit from manifesting in our lives. Lying emotions are human reactions to situations whereby we cast aside Fruits, and *feel* and operate from our base emotions. We function reactively. We aren't thinking or walking in the Spirit.

Tapping helps retake our thoughts captive for our Lord. The quicker we tap and get our thoughts back on God's track, the sooner we can get back into God's presence and experience His Fruit.

Are you confusing the world's fleeting positive emotions for God's unconditional Fruit from His Spirit?

**Action:** By our Fruit is how we are to recognize one another. While tapping on the acupressure points focus on each of these Fruits, one at a time per round, and allow yourself to connect more deeply, acknowledging that they are not emotions but unconditional blessings of walking in the Spirit.

**Prayer:** *Thank you, God, You have given us Your Holy Spirit to lead us into all truth and to show us how to walk in the abundance of all that is from You. Your love, joy, peace, forbearance, kindness, goodness, faithfulness, gentleness and self-control are our eternal blessings, free for us to walk in. Amen*

**Further Meditation:** Nehemiah 8:10, 1 Corinthians 13, John 14:27

*Cathy Corbett Reiling*

# 19

# Generations

GOD passed in front of him and called out, "GOD, GOD, a God of mercy and grace, endlessly patient, so much love, so deeply true loyal in love for a thousand generations, forgiving iniquity, rebellion, and sin. Still, he doesn't ignore sin. He holds sons and grandsons responsible for a father's sins to the third and even fourth generation."

Exodus 34:6-7 (The Message)

This text states the deep love and incredible patience our Lord has for us, His children, doubtlessly no different than we have for our children. He shows continuous mercy to sinners, and bestows riches, which never run out. He forgives iniquities, transgressions, and sins, as His mercy and grace reach to eternity. God holds His anger, awaiting our repentance, continuing in His unchanging nature, abounding in loyalty, grace, mercy, kindness and faithfulness.

However, He doesn't allow sin to go on forever. He doesn't call the guilty innocent nor does He allow sin to reign unchecked, as His mercy eventually comes to an end. God allows the consequences to pass to future generations. Some life residues are our own doing; others may be the result of our forefathers. Either way these problems intrude on our lives.

The field of epigenetics appears to show that this damage can be imprinted on our DNA and carried forward for three generations, beginning to fade by the fourth generation. I enjoy science proving Scripture, don't you?

Consequences of old behaviors appear to be literally stuck in our genes, but God may have given us respite for generational sin – tapping.

The faithfulness of our Father astounds me. Not only has He sent Jesus to atone for our sins, but He has also given us tapping to ameliorate generational curses, IF we repent.

**Thought:** What family sayings have come down through your generations? Do they hold any significance to you? Do they *feel* like jinxes on your life? Is there a particular memory where this played out in your life? As you tap and pray, ask the Holy Spirit specifically what negative emotions these sayings elicit in you.

***Prayer:*** *Holy Spirit, You know everything about me and my ancestry. You sustained us all throughout the centuries. Show me the patterns and rituals that may not have been pleasing to you, assisting me to remove them from my life. I no longer want to carry them forward to future generations. Cleanse me, Lord, so that I may serve you faithfully to the end of my days. In Jesus' holy name. Amen.*

**Further Meditation:** Psalm 89:28, Numbers 14:18, John 8:32, Hosea 4:6

*Sherrie Rice Smith*

# 20

# Give Thanks with a Grateful Heart

**Give thanks to the Lord for He is good, His Love endures forever.**

1 Chronicles 16:34

Studies have found that gratitude has amazing benefits for us physically, mentally, and emotionally. Focusing on gratitude can pull us away from negative emotions, victim mentality, and self-doubt.

I recently participated in a three-week Gratitude Study with the University of Minnesota. To participate, we were to write three things we were grateful for each day and explain why we were grateful. At the end of each week, we were to read over each entry and see if any patterns emerged through our gratitude. What was the most beneficial and encouraging to me was just to reread the positive, grateful journal entries without any negative statements embedded in them. It is so easy to forget the little things in life and even the big things that we are grateful for each day. They seem to roll into the mundane, and we take them for granted unless we encourage them to grow.

Practicing gratitude is like a healing balm on sunny days that can get you through the stormy times.

"There Is a Balm in Gilead" is an African-American spiritual that compares the healing balm to the saving power of Jesus—the one true treatment that never fails to heal our spiritual wounds" (gotquestions.org). Being grateful is a discipline that takes practice but is well worth the effort.

**Thoughts:** Often in life we are so bogged down in our sorrows and sufferings that *feeling* gratitude of any kind is nearly impossible. Physiologically there is a reason for this: Once a neurological thought pattern is formed, breaking it takes some concerted concentration. The beauty of tapping is God does this work for us. Snapping the negative thinking patterns is how EFT works! He created it to help us knock back these miserable thinking sequences. God loves to be thanked and praised. As you gratefully pray and tap, He can change your mind patterns from negativity to gratitude and joy. Caveat: This gratitude tapping works best *after* you have done your negative tapping work.

**Action:** Write down in a journal what you are grateful for, but tap as you do this, as this is one way to encourage gratefulness to grow. Try it for three weeks and go back to read those entries again and again — you may be so encouraged you will want to keep doing it.

***Prayer:*** *Father, thank You for Your Love that endures forever. You, Lord, are faithful even when I am not. I am grateful to You for my life, and even the times when life has not been easy because I have learned so much about You. I've learned to lean on You when I go through those painful times. I thank You that your mercies are new every morning. I love you.*

**Further Meditation:** Psalms 103, Lamentations 3:1-25, Colossians 3:16, Psalm 9:1 (speak these scriptures from your heart to the Lord, tapping as you do so).

*Ronda Rolph Stone*

# 21

# God Never Changes

Jesus Christ is the same yesterday and today and forever.

Hebrews 13:8

Do you ever *feel* like your life is built on sinking sand? Is it always changing too much, too fast and you can't keep up with it?

One thing we can always count on in life is God, His Love and His faithfulness. His faithfulness does not depend on our being faithful. He does not ever say "Whoops, sorry, you weren't faithful, neither am I." He is always ready to forgive, always waiting with open arms. He will never turn us away when we come to Him and humble ourselves under His mighty hand as it says in 1 Peter 5:6, "So humble yourselves under the mighty power of God, and at the right time he will lift you up in honor."

When life is in turmoil, it is okay to *feel* weak and not up to the task at hand. God will not push Himself on us, but He is like a loving parent who does not hold back love for the child. He draws us with His Love and desires that we come to Him during the good times, the bad times, and the ugly times. He will wipe away our tears and give us a strategy to overcome whatever is overwhelming us. Take time to sit in His Presence and breathe a breath of life from the One who never changes. He is always with us.

**Thought:** Our feelings, even when we tap, like everything else in life, are in a state of flux. The one unchangeable thing in our emotional life is God. He is always the same, and He is always at work in us molding us to His image. He always loves us and wants us whole. Life has a way of fragmenting us, but God brings us back together when we pray/tap and give Him our time and our life. He is the very glue that holds us together when we *feel* our life is split into pieces.

By praying and tapping, we are humbling ourselves before God, telling Him we need help. He is always there to listen and faithfully calm our nerves. He never changes, He will never let us down and He will always be with us. He promised.

**Prayer:** *Father, even though I struggle with unwanted changes in my life, I know You are able to take me through. Even though life's changes are not always what I would choose, I choose to stay close to You and lean on You. You are my strength when I am weak. Thank you for holding me together.*

**Further Meditation:** Numbers 23:19, James 1:17, Psalms 18:30, 1 Timothy 2:13

*Ronda Rolph Stone*

# 22

# Grace

**But where sin increased, grace increased all the more.**

**Romans 5:20**

Dictionary definitions: God's grace is unmerited divine assistance given humans for their regeneration or sanctification/a virtue coming from God/a state of sanctification enjoyed through divine assistance/ gift/nothing owed in return.

For it is by grace you have been saved, through faith – and this is not from yourselves, it is the gift of God (Ephesians 2:8). God's grace justifies us before a Holy God. Grace provides us access to God to communicate and to fellowship with Him. Grace is greater than our sin (Romans 5:20) and His grace teaches us to say no to ungodliness (Titus 2:12).

Often we need to extend God's grace to ourselves too because we live in an unhealthy, but comfortable, neurochemical zone(s). We emotionally abuse ourselves as a self-protective method to keep us from *feeling* emotionally hurt by others. We criticize ourselves before someone else criticizes us, or we cannot accept compliments because we don't believe the positive statement is true.

Our minds need to be renewed in the Truth of who we are in Christ. Dysfunctional, unhealthy emotional zones are tricky to change when it's all we have known our whole life. This is where EFT is often useful as the tapping helps break the mind's dysfunctional cycle. We must be kind and gentle with ourselves through the process, taking it one step at a time to create new healthy routines.

We have been blocking His grace from flowing in our lives by our self-punishment and negative self-talk. Recognizing and acknowledging our thoughts and actions is the first step. Realize it, admit it and ask God to show you what His grace means to you.

It's NEVER too late to begin anew. Scripture tells us to be renewed in the spirit of our mind (Ephesians 4:23). The renewal process is not a quick fix or overnight experience; it is a day by day faith practice, as we walk hand in hand with the Holy Spirit.

**Thought:** Questions to ask as you tap: What does God's grace mean to me right now? Can I extend God's grace and forgiveness to myself when I make a mistake? Am I hanging onto guilt and shame about past actions, hoping that pain will prevent me from repeating those mistakes? Do I truly believe Jesus has forgiven me for my past actions? Whose voice do I hear when I beat myself up with negative self-talk?

The harsh critical inner voice we hear tends not to be our own; most often is the voice of a parent or an authority figure. The enemy uses this voice to prevent us from walking in God's fullness. Tapping can help us turn down that noise and chatter of the accusing voice(s).

**Action:** Tap all the details of whatever memories the Holy Spirit gives you as answers to these questions. At the end of the week, check back to see how God has changed your feelings around the above questions. He may bring more memories to mind, add those to the list of items you must tap when time allows.

When using the Set-up, you can confess the sin (missing the mark) of self-punishment (selfishness). As you tap, you can mimic the critical voice and really *feel* into it. Clearing the attachment to this negativity can open the door again to *feel* God's love and grace.

***Prayer:*** *Thank you, God, for Your provision of grace in every area of my life. Show me how to walk in it that I might live Your abundant life and be a beacon for others to desire to receive the blessing that You have so graciously bestowed. Amen*

**Further Meditation:** 1 Corinthians 1: 3-4, Hebrews 4:16, James 4:6

*Cathy Corbett Reiling*

# 23

# Gratitude

Give thanks in all circumstances; for this is God's will for you in Christ Jesus .

1 Thessalonians 5:18

Giving thanks in all circumstances is truly difficult. When the kids are yelling and the food is burning because the telephone is ringing, gratitude won't happen. When the bills go unpaid or the car gets a flat tire, we get physically hurt, our beloved pet is harmed or a loved one dies, gratitude isn't the first thing we think.

What are our options? Can we grumble and complain? Should we hold it in, allowing it to fester? Is it permissible to blame and accuse God or someone else out of our anger?

Sometimes God's will for us seems impossible, so why is He asking us to do this, especially when we don't even want to or simply cannot seem to do it?

The whining and discontent seem to come much easier and more natural than giving thanks. However, this grouchy behavior compounds the problem by adding more stress and negativity to our life. It also sends lots of those unhealthy chemicals from these reactive thoughts pulsing through our body pushing our emotions to explode and lowering our immunity that sets us up to get sick.

Thank God there is an answer because He is the answer. We were never meant to handle this world in our own strength. He knows that giving thanks puts us in an entirely different realm of experience than any of our other options. Scientists can measure the different emotional brain activity frequencies. The heavier more dense emotions like depression and despair have different measurable frequencies than do the lighter emotions of happiness and delight. Each emotion releases different chemicals into the body. The brainwaves created from giving thanks and being grateful produce healing chemicals that the body releases. It appears these chemicals allow us to heal in a way that is different from the way medicine heals.

By acknowledging that God has our best interest at heart, we can ask Jesus to show us how to give thanks when it seems impossible to do. Even though true heartfelt thanks are the best, we can fake it until we make it. Giving thanks when we do not *feel* it is an act of faith and it can open doors for God to move on our behalf.

**Thought/Action:** Complaining and ranting are extremely appropriate while tapping. God knows our humanness; He created us. He knows what a struggle it is to give thanks when the conflicting emotions are more natural and available. Prayer and tapping provide us with a place to bring our grumbling to and a tool with which to process and move through whatever we are *feeling*. The state of giving thanks can become a natural habit when we process triggered reactions. Process the memories and circumstances with tapping, don't stuff them, pretending they are not there. This behavior can often cause more resistance and prolong the struggle. Bring all of our grumbling to God in our prayer/tapping time, and watch God open up the floodgates where gratitude awaits us.

***Prayer:*** *Thank You, God, that it is Your will for us to give thanks in all circumstances, and You have given us a Helper to do just that. Thank You that You have given us the blueprint for living full and abundant lives, and with the power of the Holy Spirit we can live the life You have provided for us. Amen.*

**Further Meditation:** Psalm 34:1, Colossians 3:16, 1 Timothy 4:4

*Cathy Corbett Reiling*

# 24

# He is There All the Time

And I will ask the Father, and he will give you another Helper, to be with you forever, even the Spirit of truth, whom the world cannot receive, because it neither sees him nor knows him. You know him, for he dwells with you and will be in you.

John 14:16-17

I have a black cross necklace that I wear practically all the time. One day, when I noticed that it wasn't around my neck, I looked all over the house, called places I had been to see if it had come off there, and retraced my steps to see if I could find it. I told the Lord I liked the cross necklace and I would appreciate Him helping me to find it. I asked Him to show me where it was, but I admit I wondered if it had come off and was lost for good. I told Him I knew He could replace it or give me another one I would love just as much - I gave the lost item to Him. Later that day I found it in a spot where I had already looked several times. It was hanging on my wall where I hang other necklaces, but it was hanging in such a way over another necklace that I couldn't see it.

I love when God reveals something to me like this -- it reminds me that whether we *feel* God's presence or not, He is not far from us and He is there all the time whether we know it or not. It is as if He is hiding it in plain sight so He could tell me, "I AM here all the time, so open your eyes and you will see Me." I *felt* God was showing me Himself, not just my necklace. I have come to see answered prayer in this same way — it is not as much about the answered prayer, although that is pretty wonderful.  God has shown me that when He answers my prayers or provides for me, He is revealing His very self to me. Answered prayer has become more about Him and His nature than about my prayer being answered.

**Thought:** Often when we misplace items, an emotional response results. If the item was special, we pray, asking God to help us find it. Sometimes, personally,

I add a bit of tapping to the praying mix because it quiets my mind to focus on God, but it also quiets my emotions about the lost item so God can remind me where I left it. As I tap, my mind quits whirling around and I can slow down to remember where I was and what I was doing when I lost the item. The power of adding tapping to our prayers seems amazing, and I thank God He has given me this gift and I thank Him for His presence in my life.

**Prayer:** *Father, forgive me for times I feel alone or forgotten. It is my heart's desire to know that You are with me and have promised to never forsake me. Even though I don't always feel your presence, I know You are there all the time and You are ever mindful of me.*

**Further Meditation:** Jeremiah 33:3, Deuteronomy 31:6-8, Hebrews 13:5-6, 1 Corinthians 3:16

*Ronda Rolph Stone*

# 25

# His Rest

For anyone who enters God's rest also rests from their works, just as God did from His.

Hebrews 4:10

Outside of God, there is no rest. Many Christians have not fully entered the rest that God provides for His children. We struggle and strive as if we are godless even though His rest is always there waiting for us. God does not force us to enter. Others believe we will not rest until we arrive in heaven. Jesus tells us in the Lord's Prayer "Thy will be done, on earth as it is in heaven". We are called to pervade earth with heaven. Resting from our own work, permitting God to figure it out, is part of that call.

When we become preoccupied with life, and lose sight of our standing in God we tend to scurry about trying to prove and justify our existence and "help" God out as if we are earning our way to heaven. We overlook the reality that He is God, the Author, and Finisher of our faith, who completes the good work which He began in us (Philippians 1:6). We should always be mindful that He is our very Life.

A question we can ask ourselves regarding the work we are doing is, "Does this deed land at our feet or the feet of Jesus?" When we are trusting in Him, and being led by His Spirit, we will experience a sense of peace around our day's work. When we are struggling to prove something, competing or striving in our own strength, the work isn't from Him. It is our own pride or ego motivating us. We aren't to go through life passively, but rather proactively, participating and doing as God so directs. This fulfills the admonition to enter His rest because we are doing His will, not ours.

What is a supernatural rest? Supernatural rest is operating in God's will. It reminds me of an air flight on a stormy day, but once we ascend above the clouds we find sunny blue skies. We are in God's rest when we are in the clear skies.

**Thought/Action:** When we *feel* overtaken by life's storms, we can experience His rest. Tapping on our meridian points while praying can quickly bring the body to the restful calm we crave, as the cortisol and adrenaline levels return to normal, allowing the mind chatter to slow down. The quiet place we want to experience is waiting, and tapping can help us get there more easily. The body calms, so we can once again hear the Holy Spirit. We can then cease our own efforts as we sense and listen to the Holy Spirit leading us. His peace and clarity returns, and right there waiting is His rest, as always.

What job or chore in life causes you emotional turmoil? Examples might be an upcoming family visit, officer's position in a community organization or planning a party at school for your child. Take a few minutes and tap about what parts of those jobs bother you the most, asking the Holy Spirit to clear the angst so that you can calmly and joyfully do the job restfully in Him.

***Prayer:*** *Thank you, God, for providing a place where I can cease from my own works. Thank you, I know I can trust You while I live in this glorious place. Help me to trust You even more in my growing knowledge of You. I want to remain in Your rest.*

**Further Meditation:** Exodus 33:14, Hebrews 4: 1-16, John 14:27, 1 John 3:19

*Cathy Corbett Reiling*

# 26

# If is Not a Question, and When Doesn't Matter

Trust in the Lord with all your heart and lean not on your own understanding; in all your ways acknowledge Him and He will make your paths straight.

Proverbs 3:5-6

My son was in need of a miracle - he had a car accident in 1989 and seven years later I was still crying out to our Lord, asking, "Are you going to heal my son because it has been a long time?" God gave me many words and many promises He would heal my son. That was in 1996. I had a dream that night, and I saw a neon blue circular flashing sign that said, **"If is not a question, and when doesn't matter."**

I told the Lord the next morning we needed to have a talk about the dream because I did not want my interpretation. I wanted to know what He meant. This is what I heard in my spirit "Yes I am healing your son. It is a done deal. It has already been decided. You don't even have to ask Me 'If.' But I want you to be in such a place of peace that 'when doesn't matter,' and you need to let Me be in charge of when." This did not make me *feel* sad or lose faith, in fact, it gave me peace that I didn't have to ask "If" anymore and I *felt* God wanted me to have peace in the waiting time, and in the waiting not be anxious or questioning about "when." He just gave me a "knowing." I think that is what a "gift of faith" must *feel* like to us.

Thought: What have you been asking the Lord? What question have you asked over and over and have not yet received an answer? Our biggest need, even over what we are asking the Lord to do for us, is to trust Him with all our heart and to not lean on our own understanding. God knows your need,

He knew your need before you ever had the need. Trust in Him — He will see you through and He will be with you in everything.

**Action:** Consider using tapping while you pray, every time, all the time. Tapping quiets your body and spirit. It allows God to speak to you. Many times we find ourselves all anxious and fearful before and during prayer, as we cry out to our Lord about our problems. Yes, He can settle us down emotionally about issues in our life with prayer, but He invented tapping to also settle down our bodies, giving us the peace in each situation to "know" and understand He has it all under control. Pray, tap and allow God to drop those emotionally driven neurochemicals back to normal levels. Let God do His God thing in you.

***Prayer:*** *Dear Lord thank you so much for revealing Yourself to me so intimately that I "know" you and I don't have to question you with the "when?". As I pray and tap I leave it all in your hands. I thank you that I can believe You and Your Word. Let not my heart be troubled. Amen.*

**Further Meditation:** Isaiah 26:3, John 14:27, Psalms 37:3-5, Hebrews 11:1

*Ronda Rolph Stone*

# 27

# In Him

**For in Him we live and move and have our being.**

Acts 17:28

Einstein was once quoted as saying: "The most important question you can ever ask is if the world is a friendly place."

How we view the world defines how we live our lives. It dictates how we react to situations. It regulates what we will focus on, and it controls what thoughts we ponder. The experience we would have from living in a friendly world vs. an unfriendly world is extremely different. A friendly world allows growth, freedom and curiosity, where an unfriendly world offers insecurity, fear and defensiveness. If we live in an unfriendly world, where we *feel* unsafe and constantly emotionally triggered, we can't experience the abundant life that God wants and can provide for us.

What if we could live and experience a friendly place knowing that we live and move and have our being in Him? What if our world could be found in Him? The good news is it can! His divine power has given us everything we need for a Godly life through our knowledge of Him who called us by His own glory and goodness (2 Peter 1:3).

How then do we justify all of the turmoil in the world - hate, crime, wars, disasters, and still *feel* that we live in a friendly world? Because our world is to be found in Him and He has overcome the world! We live in Him and He lives in us.

Peace is mentioned over 400 times in the Bible and we are missing the mark if we are not walking in it; peace is only found in Him. "Peace I leave with you, my peace I give you. I do not give you as the world gives. Do not let your hearts be troubled and do not be afraid"(John 14:27).

How do we get to peace from where we are now? Trust is the answer; trusting that God is Who He says He is and does what He says He does. The more we trust in Him, the friendlier our experiences in life become. In our knowledge of the goodness of God is where we can grow in our relationship with Him. When we become confident that His word is true, we are able to release false ideas and beliefs that prevent us from trusting Him.

**Thought/Action:** Where in life do you *feel* unsafe? What areas of your being do you lack peace? These are topics that are good to tap on. What beliefs aren't congruent with God's goodness and what He says He will do for you? These thoughts are ones you can pray and tap about, asking Him to show you His goodness. Most often some childhood experiences taught you these lessons, ask God to show you what those memories are. Pray first and tap, requesting that He show you His truth in all those situations. Once you can see God in the situation, and how He used it for your growth and maturity in Him, it is easier to trust and move in to peace.

**Prayer:** *Thank you, God, that it is Your will for me to live in peace and enjoy my life as Your child. Thank You that in You I can experience the safety and security of Your provision in every area of my life. Show me how to live with You as my comfort zone and how all of my needs can be met in You. Amen.*

**Further Meditation:** 2 Timothy 1:1, Ephesians 1:3, 1 Corinthians 3:23, Psalm 91

*Cathy Corbett Reiling*

# 28

# In The Beauty of His Holiness

**Honor the LORD for the glory of His name. Worship the LORD in the splendor of his holiness.**

**Psalm 29:12**

Recently during my devotional time, I read about worshipping God in the Beauty of Holiness which started me on a search to know more about what that really means.

When I experience the presence of God, I am in His Holiness and in the Beauty of His Holiness. We don't experience the Presence of God because we are worthy or because we measure up. The Presence is experienced by simply taking the time and wanting to be in His Presence. It is there in the Beauty of His Holiness that we *feel* loved, accepted and connected with God. In Him there is no darkness, only the light of His Love and Grace. We shouldn't see ourselves as trying to get into His Presence, but rather knowing He is with us as we are taking the time to be in His Presence. He desires that for us and He desires to be with us.

We make time for God in our life because it is just as important as the air we breathe. Sit quietly as you wait expectantly to know His Grace and His Presence. Entering into the Beauty of His Holiness, we drop our thoughts and concerns about our needs and the importance around getting answers to our prayers. There is a place where we have no need for words. He refreshes and strengthens us, so we are better able to deal with the circumstances of life. God knows our situation. In our time with the Beauty of Holiness we don't even have to tell Him about our circumstances. We can just breathe and surrender all of our circumstances to Him as we focus on Him.

You will know when you are in the Beauty of His Holiness. It is a place where you experience peace in your heart and mind. It is a *feeling* of "everything's going to be all right." Have you been there yet today?

**Thought/Action:** Experienced tappers have witnessed the fact that the more they use EFT, the closer they *feel* to our Lord. My perspective on this is our emotional hurts are like a dense fog between God and us. We cannot see or *feel* Him through the fog. As we clear out our old hurt clutter, God begins to come into view. It's not that God wasn't there all the time. It was our emotional fog obscured Him, keeping us locked in our own selfish ways, thoughts and perceptions. Continue to tap, as often and as long as time allows. Know that others have walked a path similar to yours. They have found God's Presence waiting on the other side of that murky, foggy cloud! There they have entered the Beauty of His Holiness.

***Prayer:*** *Father, sometimes I feel so far away from You, but my heart wants to be so close to You. I want to hear Your Heart beat. Sometimes it is hard to come to You without wondering if You will meet me where I am right now. I choose to be with You, knowing that You will take me into the Beauty of Your Holiness and stay with me because You love me. I can't just be still, but my heart desires to just be with You, and allow You to break through all the clutter, so I hear You whisper to me, "Everything's going to be all right."*

**Further Meditation:** Psalm 96:9, Isaiah 6:3, Hebrews 12:14, 2 Timothy 1:9

*Ronda Rolph Stone*

# 29

# Is It Worry or Concern?

Do not be anxious about anything, but in every situation, by prayer and petition, with thanksgiving, present your requests to God.

Philippians 4:6

What is the difference between worry and genuine concern? Worry generates fearful emotions in a situation by proposing some negative scenarios in our head before we know the result. Worry pushes God out, and we go into overdrive trying to figure everything out by ourselves. Worry is like trying to get somewhere in a parked car; it's counterproductive, and it doesn't move us anywhere. Worrying decreases our ability to think clearly and problem solve.

Moreover, there is a concrete physiological reason for the inability to reason clearly while in a stressful situation. Stressful emotions shut down much of our neocortex, the thinking part of our brain. Science has shown us that 70% of our mental faculties are shut off during emotional distress. That is a lot of brain cells that have gone offline! Tapping quiets the stress, putting the blood, literally, back into our brain once again giving us the ability "to think straight." Isn't God amazing?

Meanwhile, genuine concern deals with the facts alone without the added extras of the "unknowns" in the equation. Genuine concern brings God into the situation. The main difference between genuine concern and worry is how much emphasis you give God in the situation. Worry distances us from God, but genuine concern will draw us nearer to God as we place Him in the center of the problem, looking to Him for the solution. Concern gives the problem to God knowing He can and will work it out for our good. We are told in the Scriptures not to be anxious but to pray about everything. God invites us to pray and makes requests known to Him but leave the result to Him.

Thought: We need to teach ourselves not to worry. God does not expect that we skip through life without a care or concern in this world, as He knows we will have them. Rather than worrying, as we take our concerns to our Heavenly Father, we must learn to pray and trust in Him, knowing the Peace of God will surround and mount guard over our hearts.

**Action:** We create stress in ourselves by worrying. Tapping is God's idea of how to settle us down physically when worry and stress begin to build. Pay attention to how your body *feels* when situations begin to *feel* out of control. Put brightly colored stickers in conspicuous places to remind you to tap when life's pressures build. Any negative physical *feeling* or reaction is your cue to tap! God is using your body to talk to you, just like those gut feelings you get when something happening near you just doesn't *feel* safe or good. Pay attention to the Holy Spirit. Bodily feelings are one of the ways He speaks to us. He is our Intuition and Guide!

***Prayer:*** *Father, I give my thoughts to you. Even though I may worry, and that is not what I want to do, I want to entrust to You every real and genuine concern I may have. Even though emotional storms may be swirling around me, my heart's desire is to lean on You and let You be my guide through every situation.*

**Further Meditation:** Matthew 11:28-29, Romans 8:28, John 16:33, James 1:2-8

*Ronda Rolph Stone*

# 30

# Joy

God's kingdom isn't a matter of what you put in your stomach, for goodness' sake. It's what God does with your life as he sets it right, puts it together, and completes it with joy. Your task is to single-mindedly serve Christ. Do that and you'll kill two birds with one stone: pleasing the God above you and proving your worth to the people around you.

**Romans 14:17-18 (The Message)**

When I question Christian clients about life goals, I often get answers like, "I want peace and quiet in my life." I understand this as it was my desire too.

I know I wanted God to duct tape my mind to quiet it from telling me the same awful things about myself. My mind was a classroom of two-year-olds who just kept screaming the same self-deprecating things, repetitively!

I longed for both peace and joy, and I needed them now.

God desires the best for each of us. We are His precious children. When we hurt, He hurts.

He has given us a tool to help us deal with our emotional pains. In my own life, tapping has worked miracles that only God could perform. As I culled out the disapproving authoritarian voices in my mind, God's expressions of love became much more evident. I could hear Him speak. His words weren't lost amid the rumble of invalidating chatter.

One day I realized the contrary self-critical babble was hushed. What materialized was peace, quiet, and a tinge of joy. For once I could revel in the here-and-now in God's presence. EFT had worked for me! Peace and quiet had arrived. God can give it to you too.

**Thoughts/Actions:** What do joy and peace *feel* like to you? Remember a time when you *felt* incredibly joyful and at peace with yourself. How was your body reacting when those emotions welled up in you? Can you replicate that moment now? Neurons grow with repetition. Try re-stimulating that *feeling* daily. Ask the Holy Spirit to assist you to build up this new positive sensation. Consider using this new neural reaction as a way to conclude a personal tapping session, giving God thanks for moving you into a more fruitful way of living in peace and joy.

**Prayer:** *Father of the Universe, thank you for making me the way I am. There are days when I wish I was someone else, but You created me in Your image for Your purpose, with all my bumps and blemishes. Help me to smooth out the way I live. Show me exactly what I must do to attain the peace and joy I so desire. I know You want me whole and healthy, so I ask in Jesus's name that you complete this all in me. Amen.*

**Further Meditation:** Galatians 5, Psalm 65:8, Luke 10:21, Acts 2:28

*Sherrie Rice Smith*

# 31

# Judging

For by the grace given me I say to every one of you: Do not think of yourself more highly than you ought, but rather think of yourself with sober judgment, in accordance with the faith God has distributed to each of you.

Romans 12:3

Through EFT God has taught me many things. One of those teachings is I am way too high-minded about everyone and everything. Where this particularly struck me was in my opinion of others who were downtrodden. It was almost mean-spirited. It wasn't that I didn't help out with food drives or hurricane relief, but when a person near me looked unbathed, smelly, and unshaven, my thoughts wandered to "Do something for yourself. Get your act together!"

Consciously, now, I understand my mindset. My life was full of pain and I "made" something of myself, so why couldn't they pull themselves up by the proverbial boot straps to do the same?

Emotional distress is individual. It does funny things to a human being, leaving each of us to respond to it in our own way. Some never recover; others do.

Today, years later, I notice my opinion has softened immensely. God has instilled more compassion in me via my tapping. Now, when I see someone who years ago I would have turned up my nose at, my heart just wants to tap with them, giving them the sweet relief that God in His grace and mercy has given me! I sense in my heart that something awful has happened to them in the past.

**Thought:** How has God changed your attitudes toward others through your own tapping? Has God pointed out to you any secret sins that you never realized were there? Do you thank God for the talents He has bestowed on you? Can you now accept compliments easier than you once did?

**Prayer:** *Lord God, instill in me Your heart, one that is kind and understanding, full of gratitude for all You have done for me. Keep me from becoming too full of myself that I don't see or empathize with the plight of those who are less fortunate. Give me Your eyes, Lord, so that I know when to act and when to let go. In Jesus' name, I pray. Amen.*

**Further Meditation:** Hebrews 4:12, John 7:24, James 4:11, 2 Corinthians 10:7

*Sherrie Rice Smith*

# 32

# Mercy

Because of the LORD's GREAT LOVE WE ARE NOT CONSUMED,
for His compassions never fail.
They are new every morning;
great is Your faithfulness.

Lamentations 3:22-23

Years ago, before tapping, I would periodically go on a diet to lose some weight, finding all went well for a week or so before I tripped up and ate everything in sight, shoving food in my face thoughtlessly.

What happened next is the bane of all dieters. I beat myself up verbally for failing miserably. Oh, I would tell myself awful things. Looking back on those days when I verbally abused myself, I understand why I was pretty unsuccessful at keeping off the weight. I had no compassion for myself.

Isn't it wonderful that we have a God who understands that we are human even if we don't seem to get that point? We aren't perfect nor will we ever be perfect, at least not in this life.

When we first learn about tapping, something we understand could change our life, we often cannot remember to tap or we cannot find the time to do so in our busy lives. We then berate ourselves for not freeing up time to do so, or for not remembering to use EFT on life's issues.

**Thought/Action:** Don't despair. Give yourself some compassion. A little self-for-giveness goes a very long way toward healing

God's mercies are new every morning. He wipes your slate clean when you confess your sins. He allows you to try life again. When you fail to tap or your tapping doesn't *feel* as effective as you would like it to be, give yourself a second or third or fourth chance to remember, just as our Lord does. Try again. Try tapping on how you *feel* about failing. Does this tapping bring to mind a particular memory of another time when you failed? If so, tap on how you *feel* about that old memory today, too. Every negative memory you can neutralize moves you one step closer to emotional healing.

**Prayer:** *Lord, you understand my humanness so much better than I ever will. You came to earth, Jesus, fully as man, even though You were also fully God. You experienced everything I feel and think today in my life. Help me to give myself some compassionate understanding as I learn this new technique called tapping. Keep reminding me that I am growing new neural pathways in my brain and that growth takes a bit of time to make this new information and this habit stick. Lord, give me the stick-to-it attitude to fully embrace EFT for Your glory, honor and praise. I ask this in Jesus' name. Amen.*

**Further Meditation:** Proverbs 11:17, Matthew 5:7, Hosea 6:6, Micah 6:8

*Sherrie Rice Smith*

# 33

# Mindfulness

For I have always been mindful of Your unfailing love and have lived in reliance on your faithfulness.

**Psalm 26:3**

Mindfulness and meditation are words carelessly thrown around today. Let me simplify the terms: Meditation is emptying our mind and mindfulness is paying attention to what we are *feeling*, thinking or doing in the moment. For a Christian mindfulness is being attentive to God's kingdom around us all the time.

We live in the eternal. God's kingdom encompasses the past, present and future. Time doesn't exist in God's mind, only in the mind of humans. Our past no longer exists; our future is yet to come, so the present moment – right now – is all that we have to experience and we miss it all if we aren't paying attention. Our past offers no do-overs and God holds our future in His hands. We cannot be attentive to now if we are worried about the future or we are ruminating about the past.

Maintaining awareness of what we are thinking, *feeling* and doing, including bodily sensations and sensory details are what keeps us grounded to enjoy the here and now. By adding a non-judging attitude, we complete mindfulness. Reconditioning the mind through thankfulness of everything around us adds a further dimension to the process. Anxiousness diminishes, allowing contentment and peace to grow.

Jesus was extremely mindful of the people and what was happening around Him. He *felt* everything. He picked up on His disciples' emotions. He knew when the crowd was hungry. He enjoyed the perfume anointing. He *felt* the Sadducees and Pharisees plotting. He lived in the now. He couldn't have functioned had He worried about Calvary.

Living mindfully with gratefulness simplifies our life. We focus on now, leaving God to work out the details, allowing worry and ruminating to cease.

**Thought/Action:** Begin tapping, focusing on details around you. Keep your eyes open. What does your body *feel* like right now? Look at the beauty around you. Notice the color variations and the shapes. Allow thanksgiving to course through your body as you objectively view each item. What does thanksgiving *feel* like to you? Does that *feeling* calm you? Find a peaceful scene that you can attach to this *feeling*. Later, when you begin to *feel* overwhelmed or stressed, come back to this scene to calm yourself, or better yet, schedule several times a day to repeat this practice. Repetition will cultivate peacefulness because you are growing neural connections around it, allowing your body and mind to rest in the present.

***Prayer:*** *Lord, keep me focused firmly in the here and now where You dwell. Teach me to stay present with You in Your kingdom. Keep my mind and heart from wandering down that path to what-ifs and worry. Allow me to experience the joy of Your salvation in my life. Help me to feel Your presence with me, as I go about my life. I ask this in Jesus' name. Amen.*

**Further Meditation:** Philippians 2:5, Matthew 6:24-33, Deuteronomy 8:18, John 4:24

*Sherrie Rice Smith*

# 34

# Miracles in the Waiting

**Give thanks to him who alone does mighty miracles. His faithful love endures forever.**

**Psalm 136:4 (NLT)**

My son, Colby, received a head injury in 1989 at the age 19. Many people have told me I need to write a book about all that God has taught me through that challenge. I thought it needed to be a book about the miracle of God healing him, but I have come to think it should be about all the "Miracles in the Waiting."

Have you ever prayed for something so intensely and kept praying it so often that you eventually got discouraged? When God does not answer prayers in our timing, we can begin to lose faith and despair, thinking He never will.

At times my prayer to God around my son's healing has been my greatest source of discouragement. God just wasn't answering that prayer. Today, twenty-eight years later, my son is still not healed, but I continue to believe that it will happen because God has opened my eyes to the miracles that He does every day. Even though my son is disabled, unable to walk or to talk, he is happy, contented and enjoys his life. Colby is not angry with God. That alone is a miracle. And God has given us the strength to take care of him at home. That too is a miracle.

If I keep my focus on my son's lack of healing, I can get completely derailed and begin to believe it will never happen. God has instead taught me the importance of seeing Him operate every day in my life. I'm not just stuck here on earth awaiting the "big" miracle.

Tapping is a tool I use almost daily to quell any impatience, discouragement or anxiousness, keeping my eyes focused on my Savior as I await His miracles in my life.

2

**Thought:** Is there a prayer you are waiting for God to answer? What do you *feel* about the waiting? How is it affecting people or events around you? What miracles are you missing while you are waiting, focused on that one "big" thing? How do you *feel* about God's apparent slowness in answering this prayer? How do you *feel* toward God? Do you *feel* He truly cares for you?

**Action:** Tap about any negative *feelings* as related to the above questions. There are times when we must detach our emotions from God's will and His planned outcome for our lives. As Christians, we know God's will for us is perfect. Stress arises when we are too vested in what we want instead of allowing God to be God.

Pay close attention to your bodily sensations as you answer the above questions. If negative sensations arise, these are usually tappable issues. With the Holy Spirit's help, tap and find the meaning of the sensations and any underlying memories associated with them.

***Prayer:*** *Father, even though I feel discouraged at times because my prayers have not been answered, I deeply and completely trust in You. Even though it is hard to see Your goodness at times, because You have not answered my prayer, I know You are God and You are the Answer I need every day. Even though I may not get everything I ask for in prayer, I know that You know my needs better than I, and You give me everything You want me to have.*

**Further Meditation:** Luke 1:37, Ephesians 3:20, Psalms 77:14, Mark 9:23

*Ronda Rolph Stone*

# 35

# Miracles

"Have faith in God,' Jesus answered. Truly I tell you, if anyone says to this mountain, 'Go, throw yourself into the sea,' and does not doubt in their heart but believes that what they say will happen, it will be done for them. Therefore I tell you, whatever you ask for in prayer, believe that you have received it, and it will be yours. And when you stand praying, if you hold anything against anyone, forgive them, so that your Father in heaven may forgive you your sins."

Mark 11: 22-25

How we define miracles is the degree to which we can expect to experience them on a daily basis. If we look at moving a mountain by speaking to it as a parable, how many mountains do we have in our lives that we need to move? For some, way too many to count!

Jesus then added that while we pray we are to forgive those who have harmed us. In this parable He is asking us to believe we have already received and to forgive those against whom we hold anything. These are probably two of the hardest things for us to do, and they are completely impossible to do in our own strength.

There is absolutely no way, in our strength, we can believe or forgive, or even want to forgive in some cases. We need His grace to help us see everything through His eyes so we can experience a different perspective. From our human perspective, we cannot believe anything or forgive anyone. Yet this is what He asks us to do.

Thank God this is not about us. It is about Him and His will for us to walk in His miracles every day.

Is forgiveness ritualistic where we announce, "Ok, I forgive you, you may go live your life?" Perhaps instead it is a place in our soul, where we no longer hold the other person captive because now we are able to see and experience the person and their behavior from God's frame of reference.

Moving mountains and parting waters are easy compared to seeing someone in God's light and freeing ourselves from the bondage of unforgiveness in which we hold others. Walking across the room to apologize is more powerful than walking on water. When we live in forgiveness, our Father then forgives us. These are real miracles.

**Thought/Action:** In your life, which person represents a mountain? Find several distinct memories that involve this particular person when you *felt* this person to be extremely irritating and hurtful to you. Name the emotions you *feel* as you remember these incidents. Apply a SUDs to the emotions, and now tap those emotions to a zero SUDs.

Go back to the memories. Are you closer to forgiving this person? If not, ask the Holy Spirit what else you must tap about to let the unforgiveness go. If the answer is yes, and you *feel* forgiveness in your heart, praise God. He just gave you a miracle!

**Prayer:** *Thank you, God, that it is Your will for us to speak to the mountains in our life. Thank You that You desire for us to walk in forgiveness. You said on the cross," Forgive them, for they know not what they are doing." Help us to see with a new perspective so that we can release the unforgiveness and enjoy the miracles that You have for us every day.*

**Further Meditation:** Luke 11:4, 1 John 1:9, Ephesians 4:32, Matthew 6:14

Note: Often forgiveness cannot be accomplished in one tapping session. It can happen. If it doesn't, be persistent in your praying and tapping!

*Cathy Corbett Reiling*

# 36

# Tithing/Money

Each of you should give what you have decided in your heart to give, not reluctantly or under compulsion, for God loves a cheerful giver.

**2 Corinthians 9:7**

The most hated sermons in history, I suspect, are around the subject of money. No congregant wants to hear a pastor or priest tell them how much to give. There is something inherently different about tithing that sets people on edge. Somehow we think our money belongs to us because we earned it, God didn't, so why should He get a share?

Whether you tithe or not, tithing isn't the point here. What is the point is how you *feel* about giving. So, how do you *feel* about this idea? God wants us to be cheerful givers, not coerced or made to *feel* guilty about it. But He wants us to give because we want to pay Him back for all He has done for us. Isn't that what giving is all about? God gives; we give back.

Does a charitable cause have to pull at your heartstrings to motivate you to write out a check? Do you have a giving plan? God tells us in Scripture that He will supply all our needs. Do you *feel* that you have all that you need for peace joy in your life? Are your needs really needs, motivated from a God centered heart, or are they something you just desire? God does often give us the desire of our heart. Search your heart carefully.

Have you taken your giving plan to our Lord in prayer? I often receive a negative response when I ask this question. We don't want to know how much our Lord wants us to give out of our tight budget. We fear we won't have enough to pay bills and enjoy our life.

This devotion is full of questions. There is good reason for that, as money is one of our biggest sources of anxiety and fear.

**Thoughts/Actions:** What emotions did you experience as you read this? Where in your body do you *feel* those emotions? Name the emotions specifically. As you tap, did the Holy Spirit reveal a childhood memory? Confess any misuse of God's funds now and ask Him to reveal where you can streamline your budget to allow you to give as He directs you, allowing your emotional burden around this subject to cease. Secondly, tap about any negative reactions you *feel* to other questions in this devotion.

**Further Meditation:** Leviticus 27:30, Hebrews 13:16, 1 John 3:17, 1 Timothy 6:17-19

*Sherrie Rice Smith*

# 37

# Music

Praise the LORD. Praise God in his sanctuary; praise him in his mighty heavens. Praise him for his acts of power; praise him for his surpassing greatness. Praise him with the sounding of the trumpet, praise him with the harp and lyre, praise him with timbrel and dancing, praise him with the strings and pipe, praise him with the clash of cymbals, praise him with resounding cymbals.

**Psalm 150:1-5**

Are you a people watcher? I am.

While the sanctuary organ is playing a 15th-century hymn, I often see stoicism all around me. Unflinching, unmoving faces, expressionless, attached to a body that looks almost catatonic. Without seeing a chest rise with each breath, I wouldn't know there was life. Did this happen in King David's court where music, song, and dance seemed to abound?

Are you one of these congregants? What is your reaction inside when the music begins? Whether it is sacred or secular music, do you carry any emotion around it? Where were you when you first heard that song? What were you doing at that time?

Every moment of every day is filled with *feelings*. Many of us don't recognize it as such. We have no time for contemplative foolishness. We have a living to make, so we are pre-occupied. Church is a great place to think about all the activities we have on our plate. The kids are quiet, the phone isn't ringing, and the dryer buzzer isn't going off, but instead of paying attention to the present moment of preaching or singing, we dwell in the past or plan for the future. This is a mindless state. We aren't oriented to the present!

Mindlessness is a curse of humans. We believe we are awake, thinking and doing, but in reality, the most significant responses are happening underneath, in our subconscious mind, where we interpret our environment, applying judgment without any conscious input. We simply aren't paying attention to the now moment!

It is in this past or future orientation that our genetic code comes alive, either keeping us healthy or allowing sickness to ensue. I often wonder what King David's thought or *felt* while his court musicians played. My best guess is that he was animated, *feeling* alive in God's love and mercy, listening intently, in the moment.

**Action:** Pay attention to your body the next time a favorite song is playing. How is your body responding? How do you *feel*? Does the song elicit a memory? Is the memory good or bad? Sit quietly, in the moment and listen carefully to the lyrics and *feel* the music. Block out everything else around you. This is mindfulness!

*Prayer: Lord, You can use everything in our lives to awaken us to Your presence, if only we allow You to do so. You want our undivided attention, but so often we are distracted, compromising our relationship with You. Stir up our mindfulness so that we become aware of every event and memory that diminishes our connection to You. Often we turn on our radio to distract ourselves from momentous happenings and memories. Lord, use the music You created to heal us. As it stirs us, give us the sense to tap, clearing old memories that haunt us, keeping us from spending time with You. In Jesus' name, Amen.*

**Further Meditation:** Job 38:7, 2 Samuel 6:5, Psalm 96:1-2, Revelation 15:1

*Sherrie Rice Smith*

# 38

# Nothing is Wasted

**And we know that in all things God works for the good of those who love him, who have been called according to his purpose.**

**Romans 8:28**

Life can sometimes be brutal. Accidents, deaths, abuse, catastrophes, and medical issues can take a heavy toll on our emotional and physical health. Sometimes we bounce back quickly, but occasionally our emotional burdens keep us locked up in a personal cage of despair. We see no end to our troubles, leaving us wondering why we should even try to escape the problems.

When we suffer physical difficulties, our emotional outlook can impact the healing process. Stress and worry lowers our DHEA level, interfering with our healing. God gave us tapping, which seems to raise this DHEA hormone level facilitating cell recovery and rejuvenation.

Scripture assures us that nothing in our life is wasted. God turns all of it around for good. We mature and grow through it all. We begin to see others and experiences through God's eyes. We mellow out into empathy and compassion because we understand what others are going through.

Tapping sets us up to grow our faith and our perseverance. It helps us see life differently, quelling our desire for revenge and pay-back. It settles us to rest in the arms of a loving Father Who does know what is best for us, helping us see that circumstances are shifting in our favor. God is giving us the victory in all situations, even though He never caused the problems in the first place. As we clear our negative perceptions, God can promote us to higher responsibilities in His Kingdom. By relying on Him to get us through, He can then work through us for bigger things. We can use tapping to keep discouragement at bay, allowing God to work through us, not despite us.

**Thought:** What circumstance is discouraging you? Pray and tap, asking the Holy Spirit what lies beneath this *feeling* and what memory you need to clear to allow Him to take the discouragement from you. Focus on the bodily *feeling* of discouragement as you apply EFT to it.

**Prayer:** *Father, thank you for abiding with me, helping me root out these secret feelings that hold me back from doing Your will throughout life. Cleanse me of the emotions that are getting in the way of a relationship with You. Show me clearly that You are working all things out in my life for good. Assure me that my life experiences are useful to You as I move forward to serve You all the days of my life. In Jesus' name, Amen.*

**Further Meditation:** Jeremiah 29:11, Hebrews 10:36-39, Jude 17-25, Romans 5:4-5

*Sherrie Rice Smith*

# 39

# Omniscient

You have searched me, LORD, and You know me. You know when I sit and when I rise; You perceive my thoughts from afar. You discern my going out and my lying down; You are familiar with all my ways. Before a word is on my tongue You, LORD, KNOW IT COMPLETELY.

Psalm 139:1-4

God knows everything about you - every thought, sensation, event, memory, and intention. There is no hiding anything from the Lord God.

As I tap with Christian clients, I am surprised that some think God doesn't already know their thoughts and behaviors. Sometimes, I guess, we Christians think if we don't admit to our faults, sins or negative thoughts, God won't notice them.

God already knows what we think before we know. His omniscience can play into how tapping really works. Since He already knows, we might as well admit to the behavior. It facilitates our repenting and confessing of negative attitudes and thoughts. We can use our tapping time to talk to God about our faults and failings to restore our relationship with Him. I use EFT in a prayerful manner. I tell God what is on my heart and tap while I do it. This accomplishes two things — we spend meaningful time with our Lord and we also remove from our body, during this intimate time, the physiological effects of our sin and unrighteous thinking. It is an excellent combination!

Tap during your prayer time by tapping informally (no Set-Up) on any acupressure point. Allow the Holy Spirit to use EFT to meld your thoughts and intentions into His plan for you. You probably will be quite surprised at how loquacious the Holy Spirit is when you tap!

**Thought/Action:** During your next tapping time with yourself, be open and completely honest with God about how you *feel*. Hold nothing back. So often we *feel* we must be prim and proper in our prayer. We just can't let loose with our *feelings*. God already knows what you are thinking, so express your deepest, and maybe darkest, *feelings* to Him while you tap. If memories around those feelings begin to surface, make a list of them, to return to later so you can tap on them, too.

**Prayer:** *Holy Spirit, You know me inside and out. You understand me better than I will ever understand myself. Help me to be honest with how I feel about events and memories in my life. Give me the strength and wherewithal to deal with my past, and give me Your hope that it will change my life in the future. I know You have plans for me that I have never even considered. Open up my mind and heart to receive what You want to give me today. I ask this in Jesus' name, Amen.*

**Further Meditation:** 1 John 3:20, Psalm 147:5, Psalm 44:21, Isaiah 40:28

*Sherrie Rice Smith*

# 40

# Patience

**Be joyful in hope, patient in affliction, faithful in prayer.**

**Romans 12:22**

Patience was never a strong suit of mine. With years of tapping, I'm immensely better than I ever thought possible, but God has much more to accomplish!

So, what does patience accomplish for us? Why does God require that we cultivate this particular virtue?

Patience builds many qualities in us. When we are patient in small things, God moves us onto larger things in life. Patience produces perseverance. Are we really willing to hang on until God accomplishes all He tells us He will do for us? Can we wait on Him? Patience builds trust and communion with our Lord. And, lastly, perhaps the most important is that patience revolutionizes our character, the essence of who we are in Christ.

Patience is one of the building blocks of all the other Fruits and virtues in Scripture. Without patience, we simply stumble and bumble along doing the same tasks over and over in the same way. We won't accept advice, we won't await help, nor do we listen, probably leaving God shaking His head, as we would do watching a toddler try to stack wooden blocks on an uneven surface. The child will take no advice or help, attempting the task until pure frustration pours out of him. The child has no patience to wait the two minutes it would take for an adult to demonstrate a better way.

Isn't that how we often are? God wants our attention to explain an easier way to accomplish something and we have no patience or time for Him.

**Action:** Sit quietly, patiently, and tap for a few minutes on your eyebrow point, asking the Holy Spirit what area of life He would like you to manifest more patience. Be patient until He answers you!

When He has given you a specific idea or memory, ask Him again what underpins your impatience in that particular area. The answer could be anything. Using the EFT technique as you learned it, each day this week, take some time and dismantle one memory the Holy Spirit suggests to you. Dig deeply and carefully to find all the sensory aspects that hold that memory or event together. Tap each aspect to a zero SUDS. If you know how to do the Floor to Ceiling Eye Roll, here would be a great place to insert it, after neutralizing a negative memory (Here is an EFT for Christians YouTube Video on the Floor to Ceiling Eye Roll Technique, if you aren't familiar with it - https://www.youtube.com/watch?v=52GSyvzVJ1k). Always remember to thank God at the end of a tapping session for His kindness and grace in gently pointing you in the right direction for righteous living.

**Prayer:** *Lord, asking for patience scares me because I fear you will give me more things to make me learn to be patient. Instead, Lord, would you teach me what to tap to dismantle the neurochemistry that lurks beneath my impatience? Show me the incidents that taught me to hurry and move quickly, making rash decisions I later regret. Lord, thank you for your patience with me! I'm so grateful for Your love and kindness towards me. Thank you for this help. In Jesus' name, Amen.*

**Further Meditation:** Proverbs 14:29, Psalm 27:14, 2 Peter 3:8, Hebrews 6:15

*Sherrie Rice Smith*

# 41

# Prayer

**Pray continually.**

1 Thessalonians 5:17

Does saying, "Amen" mean the prayer is over? What does "pray continually" mean? Are we supposed to stay on our knees or in our prayer closet 24/7?

Different Bible commentaries expound on this Scripture by describing the meaning as having a continual "attitude" of prayer.

Was Jesus praying when he was throwing around the money changers' tables? When He called Zacchaeus to come down from the tree was He praying? When He spoke to the crowds, did He do so prayerfully?

Jesus is our example of One living a prayerful life. He said that He only did what He saw the Father do (John 5:19). As He is, so should we be, following His example (1 John 4:17).

Prayer is not just an act of speaking words to God; it is so much deeper. Prayer is an expression of our heartfelt relationship with God, where we can communicate, worship and seek Him, knowing that He is always there, loving us and ready to listen to anything we bring to Him whether it is our sadness, joy, pain, grief or delight. Even when we don't *feel* Him, He is still there for us.

Prayer can take on many forms, including confession, praise, adoration, supplication, intercession, dedication, rejoicing, and more. There is also formless prayer. That is where we are in a state of nonverbal connection with God, knowing that He is in us and we are in Him. This is a deep place where, "I may dwell in the house of the LORD all the days of my life, to gaze on the beauty of the LORD and to seek him in his temple." (Psalm 4:27). We can be waiting on Him expectantly with hope in our heart (Isaiah 40:31), as we attach to Him and fasten our heart to His heart.

Life can turn harsh quickly and we experience very real emotions and reactions to these situations. David knew how to cry out to God and incorporate his deep heartfelt pleas into psalms we all love to sing and quote while praying. One difference between our grumbling and whining and David's cries to the Lord might be that David's cries came from his heart, where he allowed God to take him from victim to victor. He was a man after God's own heart and we can learn from him.

**Thought:** How do we make our whining, complaining, and grumbling prayerful? How do we incorporate these uncomfortable emotions into prayer and not get stuck in a victim mode?

When we add tapping to our praying we can move through the uncomfortable emotions and process them. We are using our faith, knowing that we will gain a different perspective and with hope we believe that with God's help we will get to the other side of the problem and the emotions involved in it.

**Action:** Consider incorporating tapping into your daily prayer time. This need not be formal tapping where you do a Set-up and tapping rounds. Just tap on any acupressure point of your choice while you pray. Since tapping helps bring you into communion with the Spirit, we believe your prayer time will be more productive. In that quiet time, you will learn to hear Him speak to you more distinctly, giving you ideas to live more fully for Him.

*Prayer: Thank you, God, that we can stay connected with You all day and night, praying continually, in an attitude of prayer. Thank You that our prayer life does not have to be one of formality or ritual, but a daily conversation as an extension of our relationship, and we can pray while we tap too. Amen.*

**Further Meditation:** Colossians 4:2, Romans 12:12, Ephesians 6:18

*Cathy Corbett Reiling*

# 42

# Purpose

**For it is God who works in you to will and to act in order to fulfill His good purpose.**

**Philippians 2:13**

Good morning God, do you have a job for me today? I wonder what my purpose is in your kingdom this day. What kind of difference can I make in the lives of your people?

Wait a minute! I am only one person. There is NO way I can make a difference.

When I *feel* overwhelmed and unable to accomplish anything for God, I think of St. Patrick, the patron Saint of Ireland. Patrick led a quiet, privileged life before his world turned upside down. Patrick was not Irish. He was kidnapped from his home in Britain and sold into slavery as a teenager and sent to be a shepherd in the hills with only sheep and other shepherds as companions. He could have said, "Woe is me! My life is over." Instead, he used his six years of captivity to pray and discover God's will for his life. He learned Gaelic and bided his time. When God presented him with an opportunity to escape, he fled back to his homeland.

Patrick could have lived a comfortable life with his wealthy family but decided to study for the priesthood for fifteen years. Heeding God's call, he eventually went back to Ireland where he introduced Christianity to that pagan country. Using the Gaelic he learned as a slave, he was able to relate to the Irish in their own language.

According to His plan, God used dire events in Patrick's life to lead him to a life of service. One person CAN make a difference!

**Thought/Action:** Do you *feel* lost in life? Purposeless?

Are you so overwhelmed that you cannot take that first step? Know that God has a purpose for you. Remember the unique talents He gave you. Name one of your

God-given talents. How do you *feel* about that talent? Can you still find a use for it? If not, how does that make you feel? What have you always wanted to try, but never had time to do or felt you could do? What is holding you back now from venturing out into something new? Perhaps God has a new plan, a new job, for you. Does that thought frighten you?

Seek the Lord and He is faithful to reveal Himself to you. Tap while you do this. Let prayer and tapping melt away the worries and concerns of life and listen for God's voice. Ask the Holy Spirit to do His will in your life. Use His gift of tapping to neutralize any concerns or fears that crop up in your thoughts.

**Prayer:** *Dear God, let me be open to the opportunities you give me to carry out your will. Still my restlessness so that I can hear Your voice. Use the talents and abilities You gave me to make my little corner of the world a better place. Amen.*

**Further Meditation:** Romans 8:28, Ephesians 1:11, Jeremiah 29:11, 2 Timothy 1:9

*Joy Heinan Druse*

# 43

# Rejoice Always

Rejoice always, pray without ceasing, in everything give thanks; for this is the will of God in Christ Jesus for you.

1 Thessalonians 5:16-18

Rejoice always. Does that mean I have to rejoice and to give thanks for negative circumstances and things that happen to me? I don't think God would require that of us when He would not rejoice over negative things that bring harm to His children. He is telling us to rejoice *IN* everything, not for everything. Rejoicing *IN* the negatives of life is the only way to make it through life, as we give thanks *IN* all circumstances.

God wants us to live thankful lives, thankful to Him for His Love and for His Son. But Lord how can we thank You when negative circumstances try to swallow us up? "Remember, you thank Me *IN* them, not for them. You thanking Me brings Me into them with you. Thanking Me *IN* them takes you through them to the other side with Me by your side. Thanking Me makes gratitude a characteristic of your life ," God seems to be saying.

More than twenty-eight years ago, my 19-year-old son received a head injury. Today he understands and communicates by moving his foot to answer yes questions, but still he doesn't walk or talk, and we take care of him in our home. My son is probably better at living a thankful life than I am; he is not angry or resentful. He says yes with his foot when I ask if he is happy, and he is thankful to be alive. We all are works in progress and being molded into God's image, even if it seems we are just cracked pots, totally unusable.

**Thought/Action:** Our bodies function and heal poorly when we are emotionally stressed. Gratitude and thanksgiving are two learned states of being, whereby we can counteract life's stresses. The belief that God truly does have our best interest at heart all the time and the understanding that He does work all things together for our good (Romans 8:28) takes the pressure off us to perform perfectly and to not worry about situations in life. While life has its unpleasant moments, rejoicing in God's eternal goodness *IN* all things keeps us always connected to Him. And it is in that connection that we can survive anything life throws our way. Tapping while rejoicing is an excellent way to reinforce positive neural pathways, keeping them growing towards God. Rejoicing helps release good hormones that help us heal physically.

*Prayer:* *Even though it is hard to rejoice at times, I choose to thank You for my life. Even though I may struggle at times to keep going, I know that You will carry me when I am too weak. Even though I feel broken at times, I know You are the glue that holds life together. I rejoice* *IN* *You.*

**Further Meditation:** Philippians 4:4-8, Isaiah 64:8, 2 Corinthians 12:9-11, Colossians 1:17

*Ronda Rolph Stone*

# 44

# Sin Steals Joy

For in my inner being I delight in God's law; but I see another law at work in me, waging war against the law of my mind and making me a prisoner of the law of sin at work within me.

**Romans 7:22-23**

Most sin is repetitive. We do the same thing over and over again, despite our best efforts to reform. Apostle Paul says it best in Romans 7:14-23. It is as if we cannot help ourselves. Guilt and fatigue settle in. We repetitively repent of our sin, boring ourselves, hoping we aren't boring God! We feel we are cheapening the blood of Christ if we repent one more time.

As I tap with other Christians, I often find they simply give up, quit repenting, and try to go on with life. I explain to them that King David understood their plight when he penned Psalm 103:12. In reality, God hears our repentance prayer anew each time we pray, even if it's the same old sad story.

Often there is a physiological reason why we repeat behaviors. It's embedded in us on a cellular level, cemented in place by hormones, neurotransmitters and peptides.

All learned behaviors have a chemical component. The chemistry is what makes the learning stick, so we can recall it later when we need it again.

This is why I suggest that Christians tap while praying, doing devotions and Bible study. During these activities, God reminds us of memories that play into these ceaseless sinful behaviors. I suspect that emotional *feelings* arise when the memory returns. Allow God in that moment to heal us through our tapping. The memory entered our body through a *feeling* God allows it to exit as we tap.

God wants us to live a joyful life.

**Thought:** What sin in your life has been difficult to break? What is standing in your way of becoming the person Christ wants you to be? Inquire of the Holy Spirit what event(s) in your early life taught you this behavior? Was there a person instrumental in this lesson? Tap out all the emotional *feeling* components to these questions. In three weeks, check in with yourself about this behavior. What has changed? Repeat the exercise as many times as necessary.

**Prayer:** *Lord, free me from myself by helping me get out of my own way. I need to learn to rest in You, knowing You have forgotten my sin once I confess it to You. I desire Your help in changing my behaviors to ones that honor You. Show me exactly what to tap on to accomplish that. I ask this in Jesus' name. Amen.*

**Further Meditation:** Romans 7:14-23, Romans 6:1-11, Colossians 2:3, Ephesians 2:1-10

*Sherrie Rice Smith*

# 45

## Distress or De-Stress

**Cast all your anxiety on Him because He cares for you.**

**1 Peter 5:7**

The Lord puts before us life and death, and we are told to choose Life. Choosing life is choosing to de-stress instead of living in distress. Stress has fatal consequences for our bodies. Science has shown that to us.

We all have stress. It is just some of us are better at living above the stress instead of letting the stressful situations get us down. We are stressed, not because of the events that seem to keep happening, but because of the way we think about things - what our mindset is as we ponder the memories or consider the future. We mull life based upon the things we were told when we were a child — whether the concepts were true or false, we believed them.

Thankfully we can change our mindset with God's help. Tapping and prayer will help clear the faulty thinking and false beliefs. We can then choose the true beliefs that bring us life.

What false beliefs are you living under? These viewpoints can be about anything in life. It is time to find them and to let them go. Tapping helps to open our heart to let the Holy Spirit whisper into our spirit and soul, changing those beliefs that are not beneficial to us or built on His Truth.

How do we de-stress? Take some time every day to dispel distress. Don't keep letting it pile up, one stress upon another. God says we are to come to Him and give Him our burdens.

The combination of prayer/tapping quiets our heart and allows our spirit to hear what the Lord is saying.

A possible set-up statement could be: "Lord, even though I am feeling stressed, I choose to let go and be refreshed in your presence. Even though (you name what has been stressful) I want to be obedient to Your Word and follow Your ways. I know these things have not taken You by surprise and you are more than able to carry them for me, and I don't have to handle them. Lord, even though I have allowed worry and introspection to run my life until now, I confess this obsession to You and ask that you help me rely on and trust You for all aspects of my life because Scripture says I am a conqueror in You."

**Action:** Do several rounds using the basic recipe points, naming the events or the emotions. Each time you name one realize you are casting your burden on the Lord as Scripture says. Jesus cares for you, and He desires to carry these emotions for us.

***Prayer:*** *Father, I thank you that I can cast my care onto Jesus. I thank you that You are bigger than any of my problems and You can handle them better than I can. They are too much for me to carry and I give them to You. Thank you for Your love and compassion toward me.*

**Further Meditation:** Psalm 55:22, Deuteronomy 30:15-20, Philippians 4:6-7, Proverbs 12:25, Romans 8:31-39

*Ronda Rolph Stone*

# 46

# Struggle

If someone dies, will they live again?
All the days of my hard service
I will wait for my renewal to come.

Job 14:14

Job surely did have a rough time in life, didn't he? As much as I see my own life a struggle, I cannot imagine living as Job did, yet he survived and later thrived.

As I tap with women of faith and with women who claim no belief in the living Christ, I witness how much more quickly Christians tend to heal.

I believe having hope that, in spite of life's struggles, whether emotional, mental or physical, there is always a Light at the end of the tunnel moves the pain along faster. Heaven awaits us that persevere through to the end. We have a God who wants to bless us and help us heal quicker.

Now, with tapping, I know God is offering us another gift, something to relieve us until we are called home to heaven. Job could have benefited from EFT!

The Holy Spirit knows and understands what negative emotional pain we carry deep within our souls. Memories of our bad choices that now cause us problems or the bad choices of others that greatly affected our lives.

Fear, anger, resentment, disappointment, discouragement, guilt, and shame drill their way into our very cells, creating physical and emotional havoc for us. Relief for some (or all) of it may be at your fingertips – tapping. Allow the Holy Spirit free reign in your heart, mind, and soul to dig and tap out all of those life perceptions that hold you back from being the person God ordained you to be for Him.

**Thought:** Right now, what do you *feel* as you read this short devotion? Is there any physical area of your body "speaking" to you in this moment? Ask the Holy

Spirit what lies underneath that body *feeling*. Take some time to explore the event or memory He has just reminded you about. Tap away the negative implications of those thoughts, allowing the Holy Spirit to free you up.

**Prayer:** *Holy Spirit, you know everything about me. You created me in Your image. Help me become more like Jesus in every facet of my life. Cleanse me of the memories and thoughts that hinder me from doing just that. Assist me to find what is buried deep within my cells and soul that keeps me emotionally trapped in the same actions. In Jesus' name. Amen.*

**Further Meditation:** 1 John 4:4, Ephesians 6:12, Hebrews 12:4, 2 Corinthians 12:9-10

*Sherrie Rice Smith*

# 47

# Take a Walk

**Be kind and compassionate to one another, forgiving each other, just as in Christ God forgave you.**

**Ephesians 4:32**

I love to walk. Often I use the time to commune with my Lord in prayer. Nature, fresh air, and solitude create an excellent recipe to allow the Holy Spirit to speak to my spirit, instructing me in everything I need to do in life. Tapping has now become part of that walking habit. Even in winter clad in woolen mittens, I manage to tap on my fingertips while I pray.

Praying is out when another human accompanies me. It can be a wonderful uplifting time of fellowship. Other times those walks sure feel like a drag when negativity invades the conversation from one or the other of us.

When, during the walk with someone else, I feel my spirit being pulled in a negative direction I begin to tap on my fingertips, thumb tapping on one side of another finger on the same hand, or I can gently tap my whole hand against the outside of my thigh, either side, right where my fingertips end.

I do this to either release my own internal negativity if I am the one who is complaining, or I tap to keep myself from absorbing and getting too deeply into my friend's issues. While I love my friend, only she can solve her own problems. I can pray, listen, and tap about her issues, but allowing her emotions to penetrate my psyche does neither of us any good. It prevents me from thinking clearly to help her, and it harms my physiology by unnecessarily raising my cortisol and other stress hormone levels.

I want to stay as calm as I can in life. Even tempered, compassionate in a quiet homeostatic place is where I want to be.

**Thought:** What actions can you take today to diminish your own stress level yet staying in a kind compassionate state of mind with others around you?

**Action:** Are there any memories you can tap about around the idea that listening to others' problems in life got you in an agitated state of mind where it interfered with eating, thinking, and sleeping? If the Holy Spirit brings any of these memories to mind, make a list and begin tapping on all of them until you get your SUDS level to zero on all or most of them. Did someone else around you allow themselves to absorb the problems of others? How did that action make you feel? Tap on that, too.

*Prayer:* *Thank you, Jesus, that you carried all the problems of the world on your shoulders to Calvary. That certainly is a huge help for us today. Teach me via tapping to once again allow You to carry the issues of others. It isn't my job to do that. It's Your job, Lord. Help me to be kind and compassionate, willing to listen, but show me how to lead others back to the Cross. In Jesus' name. Amen.*

**Further Meditation:** Romans 12:15, 2 Corinthians 1:3-4, 1 Peter 3:8, Galatians 6:2

*Sherrie Rice Smith*

# 48

# Take off Your Grave Clothes

The dead man came out, his hands and feet wrapped with strips of linen, and a cloth around his face. Jesus said to them, "Take off the grave clothes and let him go."

John 11:44

Jesus told Martha and Mary and the others standing around the burial tomb to take off Lazarus' grave clothes. I have assumed it only meant the grave clothes he was wrapped in, but it also has a spiritual meaning to us. The meaning of "grave clothes" is anything that is preventing us from being all God has predetermined us to be. It may be hurts we have been carrying, unforgiveness, bitterness or anything else that has been said that did not line up with God's thoughts toward us. It could be actions we have done or shame we are carrying.

Spiritually it is areas where we are bound up, keeping us from doing what God planned for us to do long before we were ever born. Grave clothes are old mindsets, old ways of thinking that no longer serve us or they are false beliefs about ourselves, our abilities, our relationships or about the world in general in which we live. Grave clothes is a way of thinking, a state of mind, a state of being; it may be things of the past that keep us bound, limiting beliefs in what God can and will do.

How are you limiting yourself? How might you be limiting others around you? What grave clothes are you wearing that are preventing you from being all God has predesigned you to be?

**Thought:** As you tap, asking for the Holy Spirit's help as He sheds light on this devotional thought, ask yourself these questions: Where did I learn this limiting belief about myself? What situation was happening when this belief came into my mind? What words did I say to myself, perhaps a vow, to prevent this situation from ever happening to me again? What other safety factors or protective behav-

111

iors have I put into place around my life years ago to shield me, but ones that now block me from stepping out doing what God has asked me to do?

**Action:** All of these answers are wonderful ideas for tapping. Go find the event or memories that underpin these answers and tap away the emotional blocks you find.

*Prayer:* *Father, I ask for You to forgive me for wearing grave clothes when you have given me a beautiful bride's dress to wear. As I pray and tap, I give you my grave clothes of _____. Forgive me for wrong thinking about other people and for judging them when You want me to help them remove their grave clothes and encourage them to be all that You want them to be. I ask this in Jesus' holy name. Amen*

**Further Meditation:** John 7:38-39, 2 Corinthians 5:17, Psalm 103, 1 John 1:

*Ronda Rolph Stone*

# 49

# Thanksgiving

**For everything God created is good, and nothing is to be rejected if it is received with thanksgiving, because it is consecrated by the word of God and prayer.**

1 Timothy 4: 4-5

Giving thanks when life is rough seems like a paradoxical concept. We equate thanksgiving with joyfulness and excitement, not hardship and terror, so why would we want to entertain this thought, let alone practice it?

God speaks of giving thanks multiple times in Scriptures. It appears He is serious about the idea.

Gratitude changes *how we feel* - it shifts us from *feeling* sorry for ourselves, focusing on us, to making God the focal point of our attention. As we give thanks for situations we find ourselves in, we are witnessing to our Lord that we trust Him to get us through the present trouble. Thanksgiving is a reaffirmation of faith in the goodness of God and the care He takes of us.

As I tap with clients, there are some who still believe God makes bad things happen to us. The above text states clearly that everything God creates is good. It is sin in the world that disrupts this goodness. It's not God. God is righteous, spotless, acting in pure justice. It would be against His nature to create anything substandard. We know Jesus is the same yesterday, today, and tomorrow. God never changes.

Step into a thankful mode, purposefully, the next time you feel crestfallen or pessimistic. It won't come naturally. Obey God. Be thankful in everything. Watch your melancholy mood change.

**Thought/Action:** Begin tapping. Ask the Holy Spirit to reveal two different memories to you – one where you *felt* incredibly thankful. As you re-experience this memory now, what do you *feel* and where in your body do you *feel* it? Describe it in detail to yourself. Keep tapping. Now, ask the Holy Spirit for the second memory. This one is a circumstance that you cannot possibly *feel* thankful for. Tap out the negative parts of this terrible memory, and once that is finished ask the Holy Spirit to assist you in applying the thankful feelings of the first memory to this now neutralized bad memory. This is memory reconsolidation. Research seems to show now that we can replace old memories with new ones. Take the time to repeat this process several times to get the new *feeling* to stick. Go back in a week and re-examine the old memory. Has memory changed for the better? If so, use this new thankful *feeling*, applying it to other old memories, too.

**Prayer:** *Holy Spirit, You know everything that has ever happened to me. Find the pivotal memories that I need to tap to change my life into one that is more thankful. I need an attitude adjustment. You are always with me no matter what is happening around me. I'm grateful for all that You do in my life. In Jesus' name. Amen.*

**Further Meditation:** Psalm 107:8-9, 2 Corinthians 4: 15-16, Colossians 3:16-17, 1 Thessalonians 5:18

*Sherrie Rice Smith*

# 50

# Tree of Life

The LORD God made all kinds of trees grow out of the ground-trees that were pleasing to the eye and good for food. In the middle of the garden were the tree of life and the tree of the knowledge of good and evil.

Genesis 2:9

Like Adam and Eve, how many times will we be sucked into the deception that carnal knowledge from the tree of good and evil is going to somehow satisfy us? Often we think we can find true life and happiness from the tree of the knowledge of good and evil only to find ourselves spinning our wheels, stuck in life because we have left God out of our decisions.

Jesus said, "I am the way, the truth and the Life" (John 14:6). He is the Tree of Life on whose fruit we can dine.

Taste and see that the Lord is good (Psalm 34:8). Dining on the fruit of knowledge keeps us stuck in dualism where try to live and make decisions based on our human emotions. Feasting from the Tree of Life keeps us satisfied and judgment free as we see life through God's eyes.

There is a Chinese story of a farmer who used an old horse to till his fields. One day, the horse escaped into the hills, and when the farmer's neighbors sympathized with the old man over his bad luck, the farmer replied, "Bad luck? Good luck? Only God knows." A week later, the horse returned with a herd of horses from the hills and this time the neighbors congratulated the farmer on his good luck. His reply was, "Good luck? Bad luck? Only God knows."

Then when the farmer's son was attempting to tame one of the wild horses, he fell off its back and broke his leg. Everyone thought this very bad luck. Not the farmer, whose only reaction was, "Good luck? Bad luck? Only God knows."

Some weeks later the army marched into the village and conscripted every able-bodied youth they found there. When they saw the farmer's son with his broken leg, they let him off. Now was that good luck or bad luck? Only God knows.

Everything that seems, on the surface, to be an evil may be a good in disguise. And everything that seems good on the surface may really be an evil. So we are wise when we leave it to God to decide what good fortune or misfortune is, and thank Him that all things turn out for good with those who love Him (Author Unknown).

**Thought/Action:** What areas of your life are you wrestling with the carnal fruit from the tree of knowledge of good and evil? When we tap on these areas of resistance, where we feel we cannot change or perhaps don't want to change, we can clear the attachments to earthly things that God hasn't chosen for us, and get to a place of dining off of the Tree of Life; stepping back into the will of the Father. If struggling with life's choices has finally bored you to death, there is another place you can go: to God in prayer and tapping - it's like taking your first breath. Tap on the points, confess the struggle as you tap, and allow the shift of hearing what the Tree of Life would say to you.

***Prayer:*** *God, help us discern the difference of knowledge of good and evil vs. Life. Only Your Life satisfies; there is no life outside of You. Help me to know when I am up the wrong tree and by Your grace bring me back to Life in You where I belong. Amen.*

**Further Meditation:** Proverbs 18:21, 1 Kings 3 1-14, Romans 8:2

*Cathy Corbett Reiling*

# 51

# Trust

Trust in the Lᴏʀᴅ ᴡɪᴛʜ ᴀʟʟ ʏᴏᴜʀ ʜᴇᴀʀᴛ ᴀɴᴅ ʟᴇᴀɴ ɴᴏᴛ ᴏɴ ʏᴏᴜʀ ᴏᴡɴ ᴜɴᴅᴇʀ-
sᴛᴀɴᴅɪɴɢ; in all your ways submit to Him, and he will make your paths straight.

**Proverbs 3:5-6**

This is a great idea, but I have always wondered how in the world I was supposed
to actually accomplish this. I know I should trust God in all things, allowing Him
to run my life and I believe the promise of Romans 8:28 that He will work all
things out for my good by straightening out my paths, but I still fall back into my
old habit of worry and rumination.

Worry and rumination are sinful habits. Both negate God's promises to us. Worry
concerns itself about tomorrow while rumination emphasizes past events and
memories. Both are based on our perceptions of what life has dealt us in the past;
therefore, we assume we will think or feel the same way in the future.

Ruminating gives way to over-thinking about how we have been treated by others. Once those perceptions are planted, we expect more of the same treatment.
We presuppose our future situation will exactly match what we have experienced
in the past. It then becomes a self-fulfilling prophecy because our neurochemicals
drive our life to make those situations repeat themselves – it is all physiology!

This is where tapping can often excel. As we tap away our negative memories
of childhood, allowing God to pull out the emotional content in them, we can
then find ourselves with a different outlook on life. We no longer expect the same
behavior from others around us. We open up for ourselves the possibility that
dealings can be different the next time.

God often uses tapping to help us build our trust in Him because there is a new
piece of scientific research that tells us that for every hour we dwell on a thought
(positive or negative) we double our neural pathways around it (Dr. Eric Kandel,

Nobel Prize in Medicine, 2000). The more we trust God and others, the stronger those same trusting neural paths become.

**Thought:** What personal worry do you find the most irritating? As you tap, ask the Holy Spirit where this worry began? How old were you? Who taught you that this habit was true or a good way to act? Tap all the aspects around this worry, allowing God to prune out the negative neural bundles that keep this habit firmly in place for you, freeing you to trust Him more.

***Prayer:*** *Lord, free me from my sin of worry, as I confess and repent of it right now. Teach me to trust in You. I want You to be the Master of my life, allowing me to look to the future, not the past, as I step into Your kingdom to serve and honor You.*

**Further Meditation:** Mark 11:24, Romans 15:13, 2 Corinthians 5:7, Proverbs 16:3

*Sherrie Rice Smith*

# 52

# Who We Are in Christ

**So in Christ Jesus you are all children of God through faith.**

**Galatians 3:26**

My self-esteem level was so low that any criticism by anyone sent me into a tail-spin of despair, dejection, disappointment (in myself), displeasure and defeat. The unfortunate part was I was genuinely trying to make people around me happy, but as it usually happens when taking the advice of one adult, and implementing it, I gained the disapproval of another because that advice wasn't the sentiment of the second adult.

This all made me into a quiet, shy, rather introverted and certainly self-absorbed child who was constantly stressed, as I attempted to figure out who I needed to please at any given moment to avoid criticism. It was a tough, tiring job. And I did this for decades well into my adult years, never knowing who I could trust to just let me be me.

Enter EFT. God had another plan, one that allowed me to embark on a path I never would have considered in my reticent, near reclusive past.

So, what changed? The Holy Spirit clearly led me through the minefield of my past experiences, particularly all the ones where I *felt* deeply hurt by adult criticism. As those memories slowly melted away into non-existence (memory is there, but it means nothing to me – memory extinction is the correct term) with hours of tapping, God simply wiped the censure and disapproval slate clean. He instead instilled into me that His opinion of me is the only opinion that counts! As He gently drew me back to Scripture, I realized how many verses there were that clearly tell us who we are in Christ. Jesus died for me! He loved me that much! I carry His spirit in me!

Tapping quite often works this way. Tap out the old memories, and allow God to

119

replace, impart and engraft new information into us. Physiologically, it works this way, too. Your brain literally can only hold so many neuron (nerve cells) connections, so to learn some new information some old, useless, and unused neurons must be culled and discarded.

That is what God did for me - out with the old negative reaction to criticism and in with the new image of who I was in Him. If He can do this for me, I know He can do it for you.

**Thought:** What habit(s) interferes with living an abundant life in Christ? How do you *feel* about those habits?

**Action:** Start tapping, take a few deep breaths, and begin tapping on the feeling part of the habits. Do your actions make you sad, angry frustrated or any other feeling? Tap specifically on those emotions first, and then ask the Holy Spirit what memories or situations taught you these habits. Continue tapping until you have cleared all the aspects found in those events.

***Prayer:*** *Lord Jesus, I so want to be like You. I want to feel Your presence with me every single second of every single day. I want Your vision for me to be implanted in my feeling process. I know Scripturally who You say I am, but I want to feel it in my life now. In Jesus' name, we ask this. Amen.*

**Further Meditation:** Genesis 1:27, 1 Corinthians 6:17, John 1:12, Jeremiah 1:5

*Sherrie Rice Smith*

# Contributors' Biographies

## Sherrie Rice Smith

Sherrie Rice Smith, a retired R.N. of 45 years, worked in areas within the nursing/medical profession from newborn to nursing home care when the Lord led her to Emotional Freedom Techniques after the death of her youngest brother.

As a professing Christian of over 40 years, Sherrie quickly understood the physiological and spiritual implications of EFT's healing ability as God created it.

Armed with that enthusiasm, and a love for God's people, Sherrie quickly heeded the Lord's instructions by finishing two EFT Practitioner certifications, writing the original *EFT for Christians* book, teaching EFT for a worldwide tapping organization and beginning the process of awakening the Christian community at large to the concept of emotional and physical healing using tapping.

Today the Christian EFT community has grown to include God's anointed from at least five continents.

This book is the fourth in her *EFT for Christians* book series. Books are available from her own website http://EFTforChristians.com or from Amazon.

Sherrie is an active member of both the Wendover Advisory Committee and the Board of Trustees for Frontier Nursing University, Wendover, Kentucky.

Sherrie lives with her husband Brad in Wisconsin where she enjoys traveling, genealogy, reading, writing, gardening, volunteering, teaching and spending time with two stepsons and five step-grandchildren.

## Joy Heinan Druse

Joy, a retired teacher of special needs children, opened the first class for these children in southeastern Milwaukee. She now teaches piano and plays in the handbell choir at her church. She enjoys traveling, reading, opera, walking with trekking sticks and, of course, tapping. Joy lives with her husband, Jim, and two fluffy dogs in the Milwaukee area. She has two daughters and six adorable grandchildren.

## Cathy Corbett Reiling

Cathy has for over the last 30 years been a lay counselor, attending, organizing and assisting in over 30 workshops, seminars, and counselor trainings through Abiding Life Ministries, International. She has taught classes in *"Discovering your*

*Spiritual Gifts"* and *"Communion with God,"* as the co-assistant Pastor of Grace Word Fellowship. Over the last 10 years, she has become increasingly familiar with a variety of energy healing techniques through self-study, trainings and workshops, finding EFT and Matrix Reimprinting to be extremely effective. She is continually encouraged with the powerful results that EFT and Matrix Reimprinting brings to each session that she has both observed and administered.

Cathy is certified in Clinical EFT through EFT Universe and as an EFTMR practitioner (Emotional Freedom Techniques & Matrix Reimprinting). She also holds Picture Tapping & Laughter Leader certifications.

Cathy resides in Poulsbo, WA and enjoys long walks with her husband, time with her grandchildren, and making jewelry.

## Ronda Rolph Stone

Ronda was drawn to the Lord at the age of 10 and became an ordained minister in 2001.

God's ministry through her have included prayer ministry team, women's ministry, president of a local chapter of Aglow, Home Bible Studies, healing ministries, home fellowship minister, ladies retreat organizer/speaker, wedding officiate, and local church work.

After moving to Oregon with her husband and son Colby, Ronda spent time as an activity/social services director in a nursing home which eventually led to working with seniors at risk, helping them stay in their own homes. This resulted in founding a non-profit, which provided home care and senior community day care.

Equipped with a love for her Lord and His Kingdom, Ronda loves helping people live to their fullest potential for their God, encouraging them in their Kingdom walk here on earth that includes using EFT as a tool to enable people to navigate through the life He has ordained for them.

Ronda and her husband Steve live in Oregon with their disabled son, Colby, who they care for in their own home. They consider Colby God's greatest gift to them.

Made in the USA
Columbia, SC
19 March 2023

14029672R00067